welcome
TO ALASKA

[mary w miller + danny yo(

WELCOME TO ALASKA
Copyright 2020 ©Danny Yoder

For additional copies
visit your local bookstore or contact:

Danny Yoder

5462 SW Lebanon Road
Dalton, Ohio 44618

ISBN 10: 0-578-69589-8
ISBN 13: 978-0-578-69589-1

Printed by: Holmes Printing Solutions, Fredericksburg, Ohio
Layout and Cover Design: Kimberly Kline

PRINTED IN THE UNITED STATES OF AMERICA

dedication

We wish to thank God, the Creator of all things
for his protection over us, and for his awesome
and marvelous creation we were able to experience
as never before as we traveled through the mountains
and valleys while singing!

O give thanks unto the Lord; call upon his name:
make known his deeds among the people.
Sing unto him, sing psalms unto him:
talk ye of all his wondrous works. [PSALM 105:1-2]

travelers

DRIVER & ESCORT

Marvin & Martha Mast

OHIO

Joseph & Fannie Bowman
Aden & Wilma Hostetler
Mose & Katie Miller
Moses and Amy Sue Miller
David & Amanda Raber
Eli & Clara Raber
Nelson & Anna Troyer
Dan & Gladys Yoder
John & Mae Yoder
Wayne & Saretta Yoder
Roy Miller
Mae Stutzman
Ada Yoder
Lizzie Yoder
Marilyn Yoder
Barbara Weaver

INDIANA

Laura Beechy
Carolyn Miller
Irvin Miller
Harry Schmucker

MICHIGAN

Daniel Miller
Delbert Miller
James Miller
Malinda Miller
Mary Miller
Steven Miller

ILLINOIS

Esther Herschberger
Mary Stutzman

acknowledgments

FROM THE AUTHOR

Thank you to everyone who took the time to contribute to this book, especially to Dan Yoder for all his help, for answering my many questions, and for his encouragement. I hope this trip will be special and stay alive in our memories for years to come.

FROM THE PUBLISHER

To my wife, Gladys, thank you for your support as I was working on this book.

Thank you to everyone who contributed to this book.

A big thank you to the author Mary W. Miller, who did exactly what I expected from a seasoned school teacher! You did an awesome job, Mary, thanks again! Mary has 18 more siblings than I do. I am sure it was not as quiet at her house as mine since I was an only child and the only one not deaf in my family.

Thank you to the team at Holmes Printing Solutions, especially Hannah Yoder and designer, Kimberly Kline, who did an awesome job designing this book.

author introduction

I come from a family of 19 children, 13 boys and 6 girls. We girls used to say that we were twice as smart because there were only half as many of us. From oldest to youngest we are: Leona, William, Tobias, Melvin, Daniel, Delbert, Roman, Solomon, Elizabeth, Monroe, Malinda, Lamar, Joshua, Mary (me), James, Steven, Emma, Calvin, and Vera. Leona and William bought their own places before the two youngest were born so there were seventeen of us at home at one time. There was lots of work, but we also had time to play. It didn't matter what we wanted to play, we always had enough players.

Dad and Mom lived in Logansport, Indiana, for a year after they were married while Dad finished his 1-W service. My oldest sister was born there. They moved to the Centerville, Michigan, community and rented for a year outside the small town of Colon. Here William was born. Then Dad bought 40 acres, three miles west of town, and fifty years later we still live on the same place. It has grown to 52 acres with the acquisition of a old railroad bed on the south.

Things have changed through the years: a new house and barn; a wood shop with bedrooms upstairs for the boys; several shanties for hunting, trapping, fishing, and sports equipment; a greenhouse; and Steve's harness shop. The only original building that still stands is the woodshed. Some years ago it was remodeled instead of torn down. After fifty years it's earned a right to stay!

My first paying job was helping to rid our fields of thistles, wild mustard, milkweed, and burdock. Dad paid us a penny or a nickel per stalk, but we had to make sure we got the roots too. We had to do our other chores first then it was up to us how much spending money we wanted. When I was thirteen,

I joined my uncle's seed corn detasseling crew. This was a 4-6 week job of walking cornfields, pulling tassels the machine had missed. This was my job for 7 years. After finishing 8th grade, I taught my younger siblings for 4 years. We started homeschooling when I was in 3rd grade. The girls would teach until the next sister graduated. We liked that we only had school September-March. In the spring, I helped at my uncle's greenhouse, then I started cleaning for people in town. The summer before I started teaching, I worked two days a week at a greenhouse and produce place 4½ miles from us.

I have taught school for eight years, all with my sister Malinda as co-teacher. My first four years were in Golden Sunset, 6½ miles from home. Those years were good for me although I still believe I learned more than the children did. The last four years I taught at Nature Valley, east of LaGrange, Indiana. Our sister, Elizabeth's, children attend there. For me, teaching is very fulfilling. I love children and I love helping them learn something new. Most of all, the peace in my heart tells me that this is what God wants of me right now.

Seven of my siblings are married. Two live in LaGrange, one in Homer, MI, and the rest are scattered around Centerville. I have 23 nephews and 12 nieces, aged 1-17. Malinda and Leona live ½ mile from us, leaving 7 home with mom.

In February 2017, Dad had what looked like a heart attack. His aorta had burst and required major surgery to repair it and a leaky valve. After a week in the hospital, he was sent home. He improved enough to use his walker and go outside on warm days. A month after surgery he passed away suddenly. Melvin, wife, and two sons, had come for a visit on a Saturday. We were all in the living room when Dad lay back in his recliner, saying he doesn't feel well at all. Ten minutes later he stopped breathing. A blood clot had gone through his heart or his brain, there was nothing anyone could have done. He is missed greatly.

publisher introduction

My name is Danny Yoder. I was born March 23, 1958, to a deaf couple. My father, Coon Dan's Henry, was born on January 12, 1919. My mother was Lucy Dan's Mary Ann, born on January 12, 1936. Yes, do the math, Dad was 17 years old when Mom was born! They were married on January 12, 1956.

On my first day of school as I was entering the school yard someone yelled, "Here comes Happy Dan!" and that name has been with me since.

On October 30, 1979, I married Gladys Beachy. She is the daughter of Moses & Edna Beachy. Gladys volunteers at MCC Connections Thrift Store in Kidron. We have been blessed with 7 children and 24 grandchildren.

Our son, Joseph, and his wife, Mary, have 1 daughter in heaven and 6 children on earth. He is the GM at Premier Metals in Loudonville. Daughter Ruth Ann Esh is a widow with 7 adopted children living in Lancaster, PA. Daughter Karen and her husband, Jonas Yoder, have 1 son in heaven and 1 here on earth. Jonas works for Holmes Siding. Daughter Mary and her husband, Atlee Mast, have 4 children. Atlee is a logger. Son Marlin and his wife, Neva, have 1 child in heaven and 3 children on earth. Marlin is a roofing salesman for Amish Country Roofing and a Realtor. Daughter Celesta and her husband, Henry Troyer, live in the Killbuck area. Celesta is the manager of the Killbuck Savings Bank at the Berlin branch. Henry is with Buckhorn Excavating. Son James and his wife, Sharon, have 1 child and live in Bridgeport, WV. James works for Kauffman Reality of West Virginia as an auctioneer and Realtor.

At 14 years old I started working at Harry Blosser's horse farm near Dalton where my wages were $7.00 per day plus meals. When I quit at 18 years old I was making $14.00 per day! We had a three mile track where we jogged the horses. He also raced at fairs and Northfield Park. I would not recommend that type of job in today's world. Harry was the owner of Blosser Clay Products and sold the old style glazed tile blocks which many Amish used in the 1960s. If Harry and his wife were out of town I would answer their phone and do the chores around the farm.

When I turned 18, I started working at Wayne Dalton Garage Door in Dalton. 7 years were spent there. 10 years at Steinway Equipment where I was a welder, 11 years in our own business Hickory Acres Gazebos & Lawn Furniture, and 17.5 years at Green Acres Furniture in sales. I am presently employed at The Cabin Store in Mount Hope. If you are in the Mount Hope area for the Air Works Sale or Horse Auctions be sure to stop in and visit the nicest rustic furniture store in Ohio.

When our Bishop, Ervin Weaver, passed away, we were asked to replace him as the Budget scribe for our church district. Ervin had been a scribe for over 50 years. Our heading is Jericho District Dalton, Ohio.

alaska friends

It's the twelfth of July
The day has finally arrived.
We headed for Mt Hope;
The bus left at five.

We head for Indiana
And Illinois too.
There are many new faces
Though we know a few.

That doesn't matter;
We have four weeks time
To get to know each one
Along the line.

There are two Mose Millers
Their wives, Amy and Katie.
The one swings in a tire;
Wow! What a lady.

Nelson and Anna,
We can't forget Harry,
Samuel and Marty,
Esther and Mary.

Then there's Wayne and Saretta,
Gladys and Dan,
Eli and Clara,
And the Miller clan.

Irvin and Mark,
Marilyn and Mae,
No wonder we don't know them
All in one day!

Carolyn and Laura,
The oldest one, Roy,
Meeting each one
Is a real joy.

Aden and Wilma,
Emma and Jr,
Crist, Miriam, and Lora,
From Geauga afar.

David and Amanda,
John and Mae,
Barbara, Lizzie, and Ada,
What more can we say?

Then there's Marvin and Martha;
Fannie and Joe,
The last ones to list
Are the quiet ones, you know.

It was so great
To travel with you all;
We all ended up
Having a ball.

Imagine again, at first
The days were so quiet.
Who would have guessed
We'd create such a riot?

The fun we had
We'll never forget;
The friendships we made
We'll never regret.

We thank God for friends
More precious than gold;
The kind deeds that were done
Cannot all be told.

[FANNIE BOWMAN]

Today's the day! The day we've all been looking forward to for a long time, the day we start for Alaska!

Samuel, Marty, Jonas Jr. and Emma, Crist, and Mark left Middlefield, OH at 4:15 A.M. The bus left Pioneer Trails at 5:00, stopped in Mt. Hope and Berlin, then met the Middlefield van in Wooster. Once they reached Upper Sandusky they stopped for breakfast, and our driver, Marvin Mast, took over the wheel.

Esther and Mary from Illinois were picked up in Topeka, IN. Daniel, Delbert, James, Steven, Malinda, Carolyn, Laura, and I joined the group in Shipshewana just before noon. Then it was on to Nappanee where we had lunch and picked up Harry and Irvin.

After several hours on the road, Jonas Jr. asked, "Are we there yet?" It didn't take us long to learn that Jonas and his lively wife Emma would keep us from being bored.

Altogether, there were 46 of us, plus Marvin and his wife, Martha, who were the driver and escort. Quite a few of us had never before been on a tour with Green Country Tours so it felt very strange the first few days.

At 1:30 everyone was on the bus and we were officially on our way to Alaska. Martha read Psalm 121, then gave us the thought of the day:

The difference between an adventure and an ordeal is your attitude.

This actually turned out to be our trip motto. It was very fitting for quite a few situations where the ordeal part was thrown in the ditch so we could enjoy the adventure.

Martha gave us a scavenger hunt paper with 51 items to find. Her instructions were simple: don't point an item out to the others (seat partners frequently disobeyed the spirit of this rule if not the letter), and it must be the real thing, not a picture of it. The first one finished will get a prize.

It was slow going through Chicago because of jams in the rush hour traffic. To our right was the Sears Tower; to our left was O'Hare Airport, the third busiest airport in the United States. Planes landing and taking off at the airport gave us a welcome distraction. We stopped for the night in Janesville, Wisconsin, having put on 541 miles since leaving Upper Sandusky.

**If all the difficulties were known at the onset of the journey,
we would never begin the journey.**

Martha told us to move three seats clockwise every morning so we have new neighbors every day. That way we all would get to know everyone else better. After devotions we sang for awhile as we enjoyed the beautiful Wisconsin scenery.

On our route to Cashton we went through some awesome country around Elroy and Hillsboro; steep hills, woods, patchwork fields in the valleys and between fence rows. Farther on is Wild Cat Mountain State Park with even steeper ridges and ravines, pine-covered and wild.

In Cashton we stopped at Down a Country Road. It's a cluster of tiny, brightly painted stores set up like a mini village. The stores were flanked by beautiful flowers. Banks of orange, yellow, pink, and red lilies were blooming along with many other flowers bordering the paths from store to store. The first store started out from someone wanting to display her Amish neighbor women's handmade rugs and quilts to see if they would sell.

As we traveled on I-90 through Wisconsin and over the Black River into southern Minnesota, the land was flatter and the fields larger. Acres and acres of corn were growing. Turning wind turbines were scattered all over. Many cattle were cooling off in the farm ponds.

Martha passed the microphone around. We all introduced ourselves and said a bit about our families and jobs and such. It was very interesting. We discovered that there were four couples celebrating their 40th anniversary; Mose & Amy Miller, Joseph & Fannie Bowman, Wayne & Saretta Yoder, and Dan & Gladys Yoder. Celebrating their 50th was John & Mae Yoder.

Southeast South Dakota looks very untamed. There are some uncultivated fields, but it mostly looks as if it's been left by itself to see what would happen to it. There are trees, solitary or in small groups; bottomlands edging ditches, reservoirs, waterholes, swales, small patches of marshy land, flat fields left to fallow, and gentle rises. Grain elevators are the most frequently seen buildings. Farmhouses are few and far between. A few old Bill Peet like barns and some beef cattle take their part in the view of miles and miles.

Next stop is the Corn Palace in Mitchell, South Dakota. It was started in 1892, as part of the Corn Expedition which was founded to get settlers to grow wheat and corn in the Dakotas. Farmers at first didn't believe that corn would grow on the prairies.

When the people came for the Expo, the Palace helped to keep them there. It was discontinued in the Depression and Dust Bowl years. In the last two years of World War II it wasn't redecorated because the corn was needed for the war effort. Sometime after the war it was reopened for good. The Palace is now almost 130 years old and at its third location, having outgrown the first two.

The facade is decorated with dock seeds, wild oats, wheat heads, broomgrass, bluegrass, and ryegrass along the turrets. In the spaces between the turrets are gigantic murals made of twelve different colors of corn. The corn, grown expressly to decorate the Palace, is dried then cut in half lengthwise and nailed to the walls.

Each year the murals have a different theme. In 2018, they were about South Dakota weather including a tornado and a blizzard. This year, 2019, they are a tribute to the U.S. Military.

On the inside walls to the left and right are murals designed by Oscar Howe, the son of an Indian Chief. One of the murals has the four faces of the Black Hills, Mt. Rushmore with a bison, and a jagged outline of the hills. One was of the Indians worshiping their two main foods: corn and bison. One was of the exchanging of the peace pipe between the Indians and the white men. One was of the white man and Indian growing up together to be peaceable neighbors.

On the front wall in the corners is a picture of a white man on one side and an Indian on the other. Next to them are their homes; a log cabin and a tepee. Beside their homes are their main food sources: cattle and buffalo. Then came the symbols for their education, a book and a hawk. In the center picture the white man and the Indian are shaking hands in a token of peace. What an amazing example of folk art!

Dan & Gladys went to a fast food place for supper. After entering the restaurant, they noticed an unappealing odor and full to overflowing trashcans. They ordered sandwiches, not trusting anything else. Jonas & Emma decided to go to the same restaurant too. They stood by the counter for ten minutes waiting for someone to come take their order. Not a worker could be seen so Jonas called out, "Anyone here?" After a few more minutes someone came to take their orders. Needless to say, the restaurant did not get a 5-star rating from them!

After supper at Culver's the four girls decided to go to Cabela's which was right behind the hotel. They had just closed the doors so they went across the street intending to get water at the Dollar Store. It also had just closed so they headed on to Menards next door. They arrived there just in time to be too late. On to Walmart they went finally getting their water.

We are in Mitchell, having traveled 546 miles from Janesville.

SUNDAY, JULY 14

**A smile is a curve that sets a lot of things straight,
so keep smiling; it makes people wonder what you're up to.**

Today we stopped at a rest area near Chamberlain, South Dakota. It is the interpretive center of the Lewis and Clark Trail. Inside the building are artifacts, pictures, a tepee, and a boat. There is a tabletop relief map showing the terrain of the trail that Lewis and Clark followed on their way to the Pacific Ocean.

Outside was a 50 foot statue of a Sioux woman, a symbol of the dignity of the Sioux Indians. Behind the building and the statue was an overlook of the Missouri River and its breaks. The eastern bank is covered with conifers. The western bank is green bluffs dotted with a few trees.

West of the Missouri the terrain is much the same as east of it. There are more hills, and all the waterholes have ducks in them.

We passed a billboard saying, "Our Mexican food is so good that Trump would build a fence around it!"

When Martha asked if we wanted to go through the Badlands, there was an unanimous YES! She said we had time to drive through the park if we wanted, so that's what we did.

What an awe-inspiring place! Truly the park is a testament to the wonders and power of our great God. Rugged, erosion-cut buttes and formations are layered in brown, red, gray, and gold rock. They look as if they had stood there for time immemorial, defying the elements.

It was much greener than I had ever seen before. Grasses covered the spaces between the buttes, and even some of the flat tops were green.

Yellow sweet clover was blooming alongside a wild pea, a mini sunflower, and a white-blossomed bindweed. We saw quite a few wild sheep, some prairie dogs, three buffaloes, and a small herd of antelope.

At one point, we got off the bus to climb around on the rocks. The paths were well worn with steps and steep places. The top layer of dust was caked and muddy from an earlier rain.

In the distance I could see a cavity in a butte with my binoculars. There were some white birds inside. I was quite puzzled as to what kind they could be until Delbert reminded me that vulture babies are white.

We had a picnic lunch at Wall Park in Wall, SD. Sandwiches, potato salad, vegetables and dip, fruit, cookies, pop, and water was all delicious. We ate in a pavilion with plenty of complimentary mosquitoes to keep our hands busy.

After the picnic we went to Wall Drug. I thought the history of how the store started was more interesting than the store itself which was jam-packed and full to the brim with people.

In the 1930s, Ted Husted, a druggist wanted to have a store on his own. He decided to settle in Wall because it fit his criteria: it was small and had a Catholic church. He talked with the leading townspeople, bought the drugstore, and started up. He and his wife decided to give it a five year trial.

They were about 60 miles from the Badlands, and he hoped to get travelers to stop in on their way. Unfortunately the store was off the main road.

After 4½ years of struggling to make ends meet, watching the cars go by on the nearby highway, that was just too far away, his wife decided they should put up signs on the highway offering free ice water to sweltering travelers. Before Ted got back to the store from putting up the signs, customers were stopping in for ice water and buying other things. In no time at all, business boomed and here it is, still offering free ice water and serving up to 20,000 people on a summer day.

Arriving at Mt. Rushmore, we found the main hiking trail was closed because of construction so the closest we could get was the viewing deck. Four Presidents stare into the distance. The granite monuments are 60 feet tall with 20 foot long noses, 11 foot wide eyes, and mouths that are 18 feet wide.

Four hundred laborers worked on the project earning from $0.35 to $1.50 an hour. They used dynamite to blast 450,000 tons of rock from the mountainside. The project was completed in 1941, with the record of no one being killed on the job.

We followed the side trail as far as we could, then turned back. When we got back to the bus we all sat on the low wall edging the parking lot until Marvin & Martha came back. A squirrel, chickadees, and bluebirds offered free entertainment.

Jonas Jr. & Emma each had a chocolate and raspberry soft serve ice cream cone. Emma said it was delicious and that it's not fattening on a trip. I wish I had known that before!

After leaving Mt. Rushmore, we passed by the Crazy Horse Memorial, a 563 feet tall work in progress. Crazy Horse is astride his horse with his hand outstretched to "my lands where my people lie buried".

Heading west, we crossed into Wyoming and left the trees behind in the Black Hills. Toward the southwestern edge of the hills we could see the aftermath of acres and acres burned by forest fires. There were so many downed tree trunks that it looked as if someone had dumped out and scattered a box of giant toothpicks.

Here in Wyoming the bluffs are flat-topped. The valleys are filled with hay. Everything is much greener than I've ever before seen in this state. Ranch houses and barns are interspersed with an oil well here and there.

Just before we got back on I-90 again, we could see the Devil's Tower from a distance of less than thirty miles away. It is easy to see why the pioneers used it as a landmark on their trek west.

Tree-covered bluffs are in the distance on both sides with rangeland in-between. It is cattle country and we see lots of them in the sagebrush. Parts of the range are hayfields or are covered with grasses and yellow sweet clover. Other parts are scrubby. It was a pleasant surprise to see the west this green in July.

We saw quite a few antelope already. They're on both sides of the road in pairs or in herds of several dozen. It didn't take long for everyone to sit up and take notice as soon as someone hollered, "Antelope!"

We are in Buffalo, WY, about thirty miles east of the snow-covered peaks of the Big Horn Mountains. It was cloudy as we neared them so they still looked far away in the misty blue. The sun set just before we got to Buffalo. It was behind the clouds all glowing gold and rose fire, lighting up the edges of the clouds all the way to the east.

Mileage for today is 518.

A good life is when you smile often, dream big, and laugh a lot.

We found a secluded spot this morning behind the hotel. Carolyn and I decided to spend a few quiet moments out there. The sun had just started its daily arc, the birds were singing, and the river gurgled on its way, it was so peaceful. The mountains made a pretty backdrop. It made me think of a Bible verse, "Be still, and know that I am God." There were three tree stump seats and two of them had stump footrests.

Today we crossed up into Montana. There is no doubt why it is called Big Sky Country. To the west are the tree-covered, snowcapped Big Horn Mountains. All around are grassy bluffs and foothills. Patches of sagebrush and trees are scattered hither and yon. Lots of fences surround a few homesteads and some cattle. First cutting hay is done. I guess everyone just leaves the bales where they fall until they need them because the fields are dotted with them.

As we drove past a big stack of large square bales, Marvin commented that those are uncommon. Most ranchers prefer round bales, but a few still use the square ones because they believe in giving their cows a square meal.

We crossed the Continental Divide through a pass on I-90. To the right is a rock-walled canyon filled with boulders, lined with conifers. Some of the rocks are split from top to bottom in slices like layers of shale standing up on end instead of lying down. On one side there were a few rock climbers over halfway up the cliff. That would not be for me!

On beyond the divide is the city of Butte and the Berkeley Copper Mine Pit. The pit is an open mine that is 1,730 feet deep. It is a mile long and a half mile wide. The walls are layers of gold, red, gray, chocolate, and orange rock.

Pumps kept the groundwater out until 1682, when mining was stopped. Water began to fill the pit at the rate of one foot per month. In a few years the water would have reached the level where it would drain into Silver Bow Creek. That would be disastrous since the water is deadly and full of contaminants. Silver Bow eventually drains into Columbia River so the damage could be extensive.

Engineers have been figuring out a way to keep the water in the pit below the table level so the drainage won't happen. One way to keep the level down is to mine copper from the water. They get just enough to keep the mining going. Copper is just one of several metals the mine still produces.

Right before we entered Butte, we saw the Lady of the Rockies. It is a 90 foot tall statue set on the Continental Divide.

Simon Ray & Esta Miller had dinner waiting for us at their home in St. Ignatius. It was great to have a home-cooked meal. We sat outside to enjoy the view as well as the food.

Their place is a landscaper's dream. East of the house is a patio where we ate. Beyond the patio is an embankment turned into a beautiful flower garden complete with a tiny waterfall. Steps lead up to the other side of the flower garden where you can see the pond which is fed by a mountain spring. Farther east are pastures which lead up into the foothills which give way to the ridges and peaks of the Mission Range. It's a pretty spectacular backyard view.

Some of us started playing volleyball. It felt good to spend some pent-up energy. Everyone else was visiting or watching us, and we played until it was time to leave.

We stayed at Ninepipes Lodge in Charlo north of St. Ignatius. The backyard borders a lake and has several chairs and benches for relaxation. The lake had a fair amount of ducks in it, and mountains in the distance made a good backdrop. Across the road was a larger lake, also with ducks swimming in it.

Miles for today are 568.

TUESDAY, JULY 16

Life isn't about how fast you run, or how well you climb,
but how high you bounce. - Tigger

It was overcast this morning; the mountain peaks were hidden in the clouds. The mountains looked darker, blue-gray, and more forbidding than they did yesterday. What would it be like to wake up to a backyard view of the mountains every day?

We drove around the western shore of Flathead Lake, the largest natural freshwater lake west of the Big Mississippi. It is 27 miles long and 15 miles wide. Silvery blue water, pines along the margins, blue-gray mountains looming in the distance. All of these make an awesome picture. What a great God we have!

We crossed Lake Koocanusa on the Kootenai Bridge to the western side of the lake then followed the bumpy backwoods road to the Amish settlement in the Kootenai Valley. We had a delicious lunch in the West Kootenai Store building; afterward we went exploring at the furniture shop, in the schoolhouse, and on down the road to the west.

The mountain ridges to the west were still black with burned trees standing tall and leafless, a stark reminder of just how close the Caribou Wildfire had raged a few years ago.

Coming back from Rexford, Marvin stopped the bus so we could get off and cross over on the bridge that spans the lake. The bridge is 2,437 feet long and is 215 feet above the lake level. It was built before the Libby Dam was constructed.

The dam created the lake which is 90 miles long. Almost two thirds of it is in Montana with the rest of the lake stretching on into Canada.

On our way across, Delbert picked up a half inch pebble and dropped it over the side. I counted about five seconds before we saw the splash of it hitting the surface.

Before the dam was built, the Amish in the Rexford community had only five miles to town. When the Corps of Engineers created Lake Koocanusa by flooding the valley, the town was now 27 miles away!

Oh, Canada! Here we are! It took about 20 minutes to get through border patrol and back on our way. We stopped at a rest area outside the town of Skookumchuk in British Columbia.

We went north on Route 93 having the peaks of the Rocky Mountain Divide on our right. Pines covered the slopes of the mountains. A few of the peaks were high enough to be above the timberline. The farther north we went, the sparser grew the trees. The mountain faces were craggy, rugged, and weatherbeaten gray.

We passed the reconstructed, turn of the century mining town of Fort Steele. It had been a thriving town with railroad access until a lumber fellow from Cranbrook convinced the railroad officials to run the track farther south instead.

Before the railroad diverted, a guy was digging a hole for an outhouse and found gold. Soon the whole town was being dug up for gold. People even tore down their houses to search for gold in the ground underneath. Finally a law was passed against that; but when the railroad was diverted, the town was doomed to die anyway.

Highway 93 going north provides some breath taking scenery in Kootenay National Park. The farther we went, the craggier and taller the mountain peaks were.

Sinclair Canyon is narrow with steep walls at the south end. Pines, thick and green, covered the bottom and sides all the way up to the timberline. Farther on a forest fire had swept the ridges on both sides of the valley. Tree trunks stood up, bare and brown; charred stumps were scattered around; but green vegetation was growing in.

A few bighorn sheep were grazing on the slope. By the time Marvin had the bus stopped, the sheep had vanished farther up.

Hector Gorge was much the same as the canyon with its blanket of pines and its steep walls. We could see the Vermillion River winding its way through the bottom of the gorge. The water, mostly calm, was a clear green-blue.

We crossed the Continental Divide at Vermilion Pass. West of the pass is British Columbia and east of it is Alberta. The Divide is the border for the two provinces and also the border for Kootenay and Banff National Parks.

It was cloudy and misty off and on with the sunshine peeping through between whiles. We watched the clouds drifting over us. Above the clouds we could see the gray weatherbeaten, snow-topped peaks. A beautiful double rainbow was arched over a valley. Later we saw two more rainbows before we reached Banff.

The town of Banff is nestled among some awesome mountains. Mt. Rundle watches over the town from the south and Cascade Mountain from the north.

When we got to Banff, we discovered our hotel, the Inns of Banff is over half a mile away from the downtown shops and restaurants. Marvin didn't like that much so he and Martha talked it over a bit. Then he asked, "Who wants me to drop you off and come back to pick you up in an hour or so?"

No hands.

"Well, what a great group of people! That makes it easy for me. So…who wants to be dropped off downtown and walk back to the hotel?"

Most of the "younger" half liked that idea because there was no hurry to finish downtown.

Then Marvin asked if we want to eat at the hotel or at Chili's a few blocks away. All the others thought that was a good idea. It was decided to unload the luggage and find our rooms then come back to the bus if you were going downtown.

It was quite an adventure finding our rooms, let me tell you. The hotel is built into the side of a mountain. Building A is at the bottom at street level. It is several stories high with a small parking lot behind it. Then comes Building B with its first floor at the same level as Building A's third floor; next is a parking lot then Building C which is a few stories higher up the mountainside than B; another parking lot and finally there's Building D which is still higher up. Talk about confusing!

Hallways connected the buildings; but if you started out from floor 2 in B and went to A, you were now floor 4 or 5. To top it off, we couldn't locate any elevators within easy finding distance so the luggage lived up to its name, it got lugged up the stairs!

When we were ready to go downtown, Marvin decided to back the bus up the steep slope, turning around as he did so. Then he could pull forward out to the street. He asked Steven to stand back and let him know if he gets too close to anything. He backed up slowly, narrowly missing a parked van. His passengers were holding their breaths and hoping he knew what he was doing. The bus started to creak and tilt as he kept it creeping backward.

Finally the bus settled back down, and Steve boarded asking Marvin if he knew that the one wheel had been a foot off the ground. Marvin replied that he knew it was off but didn't think it was quite that much. He knew a bus can only twist so much, and with three wheels on the ground it wouldn't tip over. I'm glad he was so confident because his passengers weren't!

Our rooms had balconies from which we had stunning view of the mountains. We could hear the trains farther down the valley. With binoculars we could watch the glass enclosed Banff Gondola ascend up to the summit of Sulphur Mountain. The gondola can take four passengers at a time up to the 360* observation deck that is 7,486 feet above sea level. Imagine the breathtaking scenery!

Total miles for today are 434.

**Joy is what happens to us when we allow ourselves
to recognize how good things really are.**

After breakfast and a late start, we headed for beautiful Lake Louise. It's a pretty spot, a snow and glacier few lake nestled in the mountains at 5,681 feet altitude. The water is the same clear green-blue as the Bow River. The surface was calm; and if it hadn't been for a light rain, I would have liked a canoe ride across the lake.

The view from the lower end was awesome. Mountains, covered with drifting clouds and fog, watch over the lake on both sides. The glacier at the upper end was half lost in the mist, but we could still see the lower part of it.

Bow Lake at 6,500 feet was next. We got a great look at the hanging glacier above it. At the edge the snow just kept piling up. It is called Crowfoot Glacier.

Peyto Lake is shaped like an elongated bear's paw. Its name is an Indian word meaning grizzly.

I found out from a sign here what gives these alpine lakes their fresh turquoise color. Water rushes down the mountains from snow-melt and rain. It is full of dirt and rock particles ground up and carried along by glaciers. All the heavier silt goes to the bottom of the lakes while the very fine dust, called rock flour, stays suspended in the water.

This dust catches the sunlight and scatters it through the water, giving the lakes their color. Isn't that a magnificent God wrought miracle?

Next destination: Columbia Icefields in general and Athabasca Glacier in particular. Columbia Icefields is the largest icefield in the Rocky Mountains and one of the largest non-polar icefields with ice 750-800 feet thick, about 2% of the entire icefield. Above the Athabasca is the Andromeda Glacier which is much larger than the Athabasca.

At the Discovery Center we boarded a bus and rode partway up to the glacier. Then we got on a Snocoach. Its tires, specially made just for these coaches, are 40 inches thick and 60 inches in diameter and cost $5,000 each. The coaches, also custom made, cost over $1,000,000 new and $850,000 rebuilt. There are only twelve such coaches in the world, all in use at Columbia Icefields.

Before getting to the glacier, we went over and down the lateral moraine, a ridge of rocks and rubble marking where the glacier had been before it retreated. The moraine's grade was 32%, but with the big tires there was nary a slip. The coach was so steady that the driver even took his hands off the wheel to show us that there was no danger of going astray or tipping over.

The coach took us right out on the glacier where it was windy, cold, and wet. We could walk, or slip around on the marked off area for half an hour. Three sides of the area were marked by a running stream of meltwater. Martha gave us each a cup to take a drink from the stream. It was the coldest, purest water I have ever had.

All of us were back on the coach before our time was up. It was too cold to stand outside and too slippery and slushy to walk around much, but it was worth that little bit of time.

All the trees at the edge of the glacier and on down the slopes were short 5-12 feet tall. That's not very tall for conifers, but that's all they grow because they have only six weeks of growing season every summer.

Once we got back down, we ate at the cafeteria. The boys spotted two mountain goats way up the mountainside. Once was a young one so we guessed the other one was its mother. They were way up high so I was glad for my binoculars.

Soon after we were on the road again, we went past the Glacier Skywalk. It is a glass bottomed platform jutting out 919 feet above the valley floor. It gives you a bird's eye view of the Canadian Rockies. I would have been willing to try it, but Dan Yoder would not. We soon found that he is afraid of heights.

Athabasca Falls, pretty spectacular. Below the falls the gorge walls are vertical curved rock. The water tumbles and rushes and foams over the precipice and on down the gorge, spilling, churning, and frothing as it goes.

Just as we were ready to leave the parking lot, we noticed some people looking fixedly at the woods behind the outhouses. Not fifty feet away was a baby black bear. Marvin set a record for a 15 yard dash to get a good picture of it. We watched for a few minutes then finally, the mother! That got everyone excited.

That was a good beginning to spotting wildlife. Soon after that we saw a mother bear with her two cubs. Half a mile farther we saw two elk. Then a 5x5 or 6x6 elk. Then an even bigger bull elk. Marvin kindly stopped each time and let us get a good look at them all.

We passed Mt. Robson on our way to Valemont. It is the highest peak in the Canadian Rockies at 12,972 feet. Its peak was hidden behind a thin layer of clouds. The top of the ridge is circular with peaks jutting upward.

Earlier we traveled beside the Endless Chain Ridge. The name fits it to a T. The ridge rose up and up above the trees, bare gray rock sheering to a razor like edge on top. On and on it went. Several times I thought it would stop, but then another section was always there around the bend.

Almost at Valemont and "Moose!" A bull on the left side disappeared into the woods quickly enough that not everyone saw him.

People were telling us that we should see wildlife around Jasper, and they were correct, much to our satisfaction.

Wayne told us that he was talking with the desk clerk last night. The clerk, a woman, asked where we're headed.

When Wayne said to Alaska, she asked, "Where's that?"

"North!"

"Oh, it's got to be cold up there!"

Not long after we were on the road this morning, Dan started looking for his travel bag. He looked all around their seat, even kneeling down to look beneath it. No bag. When asked what he was after, he said he can't find his travel bag. Then Joe Bowman inquired, "Do you need your bib and pacifier or what?"

"Yeah," Dan responded, "I didn't pack any extras."

Sometime later Jonas Jr. Came forward with the bag saying, "I didn't steal it, you know. It was right in the middle of the aisle, and I was afraid it was a hazard to people so I removed it for safety reasons."

"So you were just looking out for someone else then?"

"Yes, but you know the good part about it? It got you down on your knees!"

Mileage for today is 198. Total miles are 2,805.

**Remember when you travel, a foreign country isn't made
to make you comfortable, but to make its own people comfortable.**

We were on the road by 8:00.

By 9:30 we had seen one bear and glimpsed another. Then another bear. Another one and another one. All were black bears.

We followed the Yellowhead Highway from Valemont to Prince George then took Highway 97 north and east to Dawson Creek.

The roadsides are quite colorful with fiery paintbrush, small white daisies, and bright rose-pink fireweed. At one of the rest stops there were cloudberry bushes growing at the edge of the parking lot. They looked like giant unripe raspberries, and Delbert said they are in the same family.

We had asked Martha what the word cache means on our scavenger hunt. She didn't know either and said to just keep our eyes open. This morning she said it's a small cabin hunters and trappers built to store fur and meat. They'd put it up on stilts so the stores would be safe from marauders.

Almost halfway between Prince George and Dawson Creek are the Bijoux Falls. Bijoux is French for jewel and is a very appropriate name for the falls.

We were on the trail at the base where the mist blew over us. It is one of those start out small and end up big falls. They start out as one stream when they come over the edge, spreading out as they come farther down. The water tumbles over the smaller rocks and slips down between the larger ones.

About halfway up we saw two American dippers, gray 7½ inch birds that walk on the bottom of mountain streams searching for food.

The closer we got to Dawson Creek, the more canola fields we saw. There were acres and acres of bright sunshine yellow canola in bloom. It is almost bright enough to hurt your eyes on a cloudy day.

Oh, another moose! A big fella at the edge of a canola field. He stood there and studied the bus a bit then went on his way, browsing for dinner.

Doing laundry can become quite a fiasco: Who's next in line? Are you done? It shouldn't take too long. I'm only using the one washer.

Most of the hotels have one or two washers so it can create a race to see who gets to the laundry room first. Last evening Crist did his at midnight. It wasn't too crowded then! Gladys did laundry at 5:00 this morning. I'm guessing it wasn't crowded either!

We reached the hotel in Dawson Creek early. Quite a few of us ended up in the breakfast room playing games. What better way is there to spend an evening with friends?

Miles for today were 401.

Be selective in your battles, for sometimes peace is better than being right.

We started off at mile 0 of the Alaska Highway in Dawson Creek. Among the many highlights we have already had, this is one of the biggest: traveling the Alaska Highway. We are on our way north to Fort Nelson, the gateway to the Northern Rockies.

About a mile or so down the road passed a gigantic stockpile of logs. Logging must be an important industry in that region. Marvin said he thinks they are Paul Bunyan's toothpicks.

The Alaska Highway

It was first called Alcan Highway. Fearing Japanese invasion in World War II, Canadian and U.S. governments decided to build a military road through the Canadian North into Alaska. It stretches from Dawson Creek, British Columbia, to Delta Junction, Alaska. It was mapped out using winter hunting trails, traplines, and summer pack trails although some parts of the highway were built where no previous trails had been.

Beginning March 1672, in temperatures at 30° below zero, more than 16,000 American and British troops and civilians punched out the road through forests, rolling fields, and muskeg; past turquoise blue lakes, through high mountain passes, and over numerous rivers. They built 133 bridges and put in 8,000 culverts along the length of the highway. In just over eight months they had connected Dawson Creek to Fairbanks.

Originally, the road was 1,422 miles to Delta Junction. Now with straightening curves and some rerouting over the years, it is 40 miles shorter.

When the soldiers first started building the road across the muskeg, they scraped off the top layer to put down a foundation for the road. This led to serious flooding problems. The permafrost, without its insulating layer, thawed and turned the road into a muddy disaster.

The Army soon learned it was best to put down the sand and gravel for the roadbed right on top of the insulating layer. The ground underneath would stay frozen, and it would be less muddy.

At first the road was just a pioneer military route through the wilderness. Improvements were begun the following year to upgrade it to an all weather road. Although improved, it was not open to the public until 1948. Now most of the highway is paved or chip and sealed. In 1996, it was designated as an International Historic Civil Engineering Landmark.

The northlands in Canada east of the mountains are pretty rugged. Most of it is hilly, not mountainous, though some parts are rather flat. Trees are in abundance. There is not much agriculture although timber must be a thriving business.

Open areas are filled with shrubs. One kind looks like a tiny blooming elderberry. Fireweed grows all over; it's one of the prettiest roadside flowers I've ever seen.

We saw many of oil and fuel trucks on this section of the highway. Every so often there is a trailer park where the oil field workers live. North America's largest gas processing plant is in Fort Nelson. Large deposits of shale gas are found there too.

At mile 80 we stopped for a break. Several highway repair machines were parked there also. One rig was as long as a semi truck and trailer, and none of us had ever seen one like it before. One of the workers said these machines grind up old pavement; and with some tar added, they lay the pavement right back down again. Because the highway is in such a remote area, it isn't practical to haul in new pavement for repairs.

Also at this rest stop was a tire swing for weary travelers to relax on. Mose Katie tried out the swing, and it held her without a problem. I wonder when she last had a tire swing ride?

We stopped for lunch at Mag-n-Mel's in Sasquatch Crossing at historic mile 147. We had just started eating when through the door came a guy dressed in a dark brown, long haired, head to toe Sasquatch costume. He came in waving and shaking hands, rubbing his stomach. At the end of the counter he grabbed a big bowl of cookies and headed for the door. Scolded by the waitress, he put the cookies back. Out the door he went, coming back in with a small puppy in his hands. He tried to stuff the puppy in his mouth, pretending he was quite ravenous. In and out he went, scaring the wits out of two little girls in the process.

Arriving at Fort Nelson, we checked in at the hotel then went to Fort Nelson Heritage Museum. I wish we would have had more time there. Half a day isn't enough to see everything.

There were old cars, dozens of pieces of old farm equipment and other machinery, including a cable driven bulldozer.

There was an old wooden bus with blue paint chipping off. The seats inside were wooden, each holding one passenger. I think there were ten seats. It was a motor vehicle but it had a slow moving vehicle emblem on the back. Passengers entered at the back via two steps and wooden doors.

One building had old cars, license plates, road signs, old carriages, and such. There was a post office with only 32 boxes for mail. One building was filled with CN Telephone equipment.

They had moved an old Anglican church house on-site. Two houses were filled with anything and everything a frontier household would have in the early 1900's. One of those two was the residence of the man who started the museum with his personal collection of things he couldn't bear to see abandoned or destroyed.

There was a trapper's cabin and cache filled with anything from a toboggan to snowshoes to traps and furs to guns and knives and kettles. Behind the gift shop was a room filled to the brim with hundreds of other items. Wayne thought it was scary to see machinery such as he had used on his farm now being displayed at a museum! It was a very fascinating place.

Fort Nelson was first established in 1805, as a fur trading post. It is thought to have been 80 miles south of the Nelson Forks. A second Fort Nelson, located south of the first fort, was destroyed by fire in 1813, and its eight settlers massacred by the natives. The third Fort Nelson was established on the river's west bank in 1865. It was built by the Hudson's Bay Company to keep out free traders from the Mackenzie River to the north and Fort St. John to the south.

This trading post was destroyed by a flood in 1890, and a fourth Fort Nelson was built on higher ground upstream and across the river. This is now called Old Fort Nelson. The present Fort Nelson is actually the fifth site called by that name.

Travel makes one modest; you see what a tiny place you occupy.

Martha informed us this morning that we should see lots of wildlife today. We saw two deer and a bear before we stopped at Tetsa River Lodge where we had coffee and cinnamon bun break. The rolls were huge, gooey, and delicious.

When we got to Tetsa, the owner's wife came out to welcome us and to tell us the cinnamon buns are ready for us. Then she said there's a motor home caravan pulling in, and some of them had asked for buns too. She told them we get first dibs because Martha had called yesterday to say we were coming. She hadn't known the caravan was going to be there.

Moses found out that there were 24 motor homes, big class A ones, in the caravan. They had started their trip in May and would finish in late September or early October.

We left the flat land behind us this morning, first climbing Steamboat Mountain. After Tetsa the highway goes through Summit Pass on the shore of Summit Lake. It is named Summit because that is where the highway is at it's highest altitude. The lake has the same green-blue water as a glacier fed lake does.

Summit Lake is in Stone Mountain Provincial Park. The lower slopes of the mountains are tree-covered. The gray limestone peaks are bare and rough. Rocks and boulders are piled between the trees.

The MacDonald River flows through the bottom of the gorge. It is named for a Cree Indian who helped the surveyors for the highway. Its banks are lined with gray rocks, and it has a rocky, gravelly bottom.

More wildlife: a few stone sheep, a bear up a tree, and a moose down below us in a bog.

We had stopped to watch the moose for a bit then pulled out on the road to go on. Not even a quarter mile down the road we noticed a car with a U-Haul trailer. It was stuck in the soft gravel on a pull-off. Another guy in a truck had stopped to help them out. They had dug shallow holes and were putting traction sleds under the front wheels. Marvin stopped the bus and fourteen men and boys piled off to push the car out onto the road. The man's wife was so overwhelmed that she looked as if she were going to cry. She kept giving us a thumbs up and waved thank yous to everyone. It made us wonder how long they had been stuck.

A baby and two big caribou were at Muncho Lake. We drove along the entire length of the lake which is about eight miles. The water is super clear. From the road we could quite plainly see the bottom in depths of several feet. Across the lake are mountains skirted with trees, rising up to the craggy gray peaks.

Northwest of Muncho Lake the terrain is pretty rugged. Steep slopes and dry washes are plentiful. It doesn't look as if anyone lives there except right beside the highway.

We stopped at Coal River for lunch. They were understaffed, one person in the kitchen and one at the till, and very unprepared for such a large crowd. Not to say they only had tables enough to seat 20 people. We waited a long time for the last ones to get their sandwiches. The special was a scrumptious buffalo burger. Meanwhile Delbert spotted a black bear in a clearing way up in the mountain on the other side of the road. At least that provided some distraction while we waited.

Someone wondered if this stop was an adventure, an ordeal, or an experience. Martha thought it probably was an experience which was good for us, saying, "Blessed the flexible for they shall not be bent out of shape."

Not long after we left Coal River, we saw a few lone buffaloes. Farther on there was a herd of fifty or so. Some were to the left, some to the right, and some were crossing the road. They were very unconcerned about tourists and traffic just as if they knew they had the right of way. There were calves, yearlings, cows, young bulls, and old massive bulls.

Just before we entered the Yukon, we passed another herd of about forty buffaloes.

We stayed in Watson Lake, Yukon for the night. The hotel had no elevators so up and down the steps we went with the luggage. The single guys were kind enough to help others with their luggage.

There was no place to play games, it was raining, and Wayne had told us girls that he wouldn't recommend going outside at all because of all the characters loafing around outside. It was a sad sight with all the empty bottles lying around and more being emptied.

Today's mileage is 318.

Be careful how you live; you may be the only Bible some people ever read.

Breakfast was in the hotel restaurant. We girls had almost finished when we noticed the couple whose car had been stuck yesterday. We stopped at their table to talk with them. The woman recognized us and thanked us profusely again.

She said her husband and son are both stationed in Fairbanks with the army, and they are moving some of their belongings.

They hadn't been stuck long yesterday, but she had been almost frantic because it was in the middle of nowhere. She said it felt as if God had sent a bus full of angels to help them out.

We met very little traffic this morning. We sang "Lob Lied" plus many other songs. We start most mornings out with a verse from Martha and a prayer from Marvin; then we sing for awhile. It is a good way to start out the day.

Yukon's motto is "Larger than Life". It fits the wild, rugged territory well. Lofty mountains, rivers, lakes, forests of spruce and fir, wildlife. Yukon has it all. Fireweed is the most dominant wildflower since it is one of the first plants to grow in an area burned by wildfire.

We stopped at Rancheria Falls for a restroom break and to hike the quarter mile back to the falls. The river forks making two sets of falls. Below the falls the water was so clear that we could see the bottom of a ten foot deep hole.

On the way back to the bus we spotted a few spruce grouse beside the trail. One was an adult and the others were chicks. They scurried about until they thought they were in a safe spot, then they just stood there, cocking one eye at us and clucking occasionally.

After lunch in Whitehorse, the capital of Yukon, we paid a visit to the Whitehorse Fishway. It is North America's largest wooden fish ladder and bypasses the Whitehorse Dam on the Yukon River. The ladder was built when the electric company built the dam for power. It is a system of chutes to guide salmon around the dam so they can go on up the river to their spawning grounds.

We were told that no salmon were that far upstream yet. A few more weeks and they should be going through the ladder. Martha said that maybe we'll have time to stop in on our way back to watch the salmon.

The life of a salmon is a miracle. Responding to the instinct God gave them, adult salmon leave the Bering Sea in early summer and begin a 2,000 mile journey up the Yukon River.

They don't eat on this journey but rely on stored fat for energy. The three month trip doesn't end until they are in the exact location where they were spawned several years earlier, a location they haven't been to since they left it to journey to the sea when they were young.

Many salmon do not survive the dangers of upriver travel, bears and man being the two greatest enemies. The ones that do make it all the way back die after spawning, completing their life cycle and beginning the next.

Outside Whitehorse is Miles Canyon. The canyon is carved by the Yukon River. The wall are thirty to forty feet high. Trails lead through the forest on both sides of the river. The 85 foot Robert Lowe suspension bridge spans the chasm. The bridge is wooden, and it bounced and wobbled if more than half a dozen people were on it at once.

Wildlife total for today is two black bears. We stopped to watch one of them. He gave us a pretty good view while he was chewing away at vegetation on the bank.

We are in Haines Junction for the night. It is rainy and the mountains to the north are clothed in fog and rain. Some of us decided to move the small tables in our rooms, squeeze together, and play games outside on the balcony. It was a bit chilly, but we played until after 10:30. It still wasn't quite dark. Twilight lasts a long time here in the north.

Haines Junction is the gateway to Kluane National Park. To the southwest are the beautiful snow covered Kluane Ranges, providing an awesome backdrop to the wilderness west of the highway. These mountains stretch in an almost unbroken chain, interrupted by only a few large valleys. Behind the Kluane Ranges and not visible from the road are the St. Elias Mountains. The highest peak in Canada, Mt. Logan, is in the St. Elias range.

Mile total for today is 382.

WELCOME TO ALASKA

Minds are like parachutes; they only work when open.

It was chilly and damp this morning though the rain had stopped. Quite a few of our crowd went to the gas station to get something for breakfast. When Eli Rabers came back, someone asked if he found something to eat. "Well," he responded, "I saw a few crows flying about!"

For fifty miles we drove along the eastern edge of Kluane National Park. We stopped for a few minutes at the Tachal Dhal Visitor Center to see if they were spotting any sheep up in the mountains. They hadn't seen any so we went on.

Kluane Lake was to our right and the park to our left. The lake is the largest lake in the Yukon with an area of 154 square miles. It has a spectacular backdrop of mountains on all sides. The sunbeams were sifting golden light down through the clouds. The water's surface was smooth as a mirror. A layer of fog hung over the lake turning the water a cool silvery blue. To our left we spotted a few sheep up so high we couldn't see them very well even with binoculars.

The center of the park holds the highest mountains in Canada, swathed in a vast field of ice, snow, and glaciers. Bare and windswept, the outer mountains offer a harsh environment for the sheep; but somehow they manage to survive.

Despite the harshness of the glaciers and ice above, that is what the boreal forests farther down need to survive. They need the moisture from melting snow and ice in summer to grow. The ice field has to be vast and deep to stay frozen underneath during the summer so the moisture doesn't ever come to an end.

We stopped at the Kluane Museum in Burwash Landing. Outside is the world's largest gold pan. It is 28 feet across and sports the village name in golden letters.

Inside the museum is several hours worth of exploring. There are dozens of excellent wildlife displays: wolverines, beaver, lynx, fisher, marten, snowshoe hares, ptarmigan, mallards, pintails, a loon, great horned owl, boreal owl, magpie, ravens, black bears, grizzlies, polar bears, wolves, coyotes, moose, barrenland and mountain caribou, spruce grouse, ruffed grouse, seal, and red foxes are along both sides of the corridor.

In the center of the display room were a Swainson's hawk, snowy owls, golden eagles, a bald eagle, Dall sheep, bighorn sheep, and mountain goats.

One part held all their native First Nation artifacts: beaded moccasins, necklaces, headbands, mukluks, tunics, and parkas. Arrows, adzes, fleshing and skinning knives, a moose call, a moose hide boat, a baby carrier, hunting bags, spears, and spearheads were also displayed.

The moose call was a scapula, or shoulder bone, of a moose. By rubbing it against a tree, the natives made it sound as if a bull moose was making a scrape. This lured a moose within hearing distance to come investigate, hopefully coming close enough to be shot or speared.

The boat was made from two raw moose hides sewn together with sinew. The seams were sealed with pitch and bear or moose grease. Then the hides were stretched over a framework of willow and tied down with rawhide strips. Once the boat was used for a while, the hides could be taken off. Since they were softened by use in water, they could be tanned and made into clothing. If the boat was kept where it stayed damp, one set of hides could be used for two years.

On the road again, bear! A grizzly! It crossed the road ahead of us and had disappeared in the brush and trees by the time we came to the spot.

We came upon a semi truck that had tumbled into the ravine at the side of the road. It was bashed up pretty bad and lying on its side. Marvin went down to check if anyone needed help. He couldn't find anyone around so we just went on, hoping the driver made it out alive.

South of Beaver Creek we drove through a big burned out area. In several places the fire had jumped the highway and burned away on the east side of it. Talk about a stark, naked landscape! The firs and spruce were burned brown poles, the ground was charred black, looked like wet clay. The road had been closed, but the rain yesterday had helped to quench the fire. Small plumes of smoke were still rising here and there in the hazy air.

We had lunch in Beaver Creek at Buckshot Betty's. The soup and sandwiches were good; the service not so much. There were not enough workers and they didn't have enough lunch prepared for us. A few orders got mixed up or forgotten. They had been very busy the past few days feeding firefighters who had come to put out the area fires. I can imagine they felt a little overwhelmed with a bus full of people dropping in on top of that.

At 2:40 we arrived at the Alaska welcome sign at MP 1,189. How wonderful to finally actually be here! To be standing on the border between two wild, remote lands. All of us got off to savor the moment.

The Canada-Alaska border follows the 141st meridian for 600 miles, all the way from the Arctic Ocean south to the St. Elias Mountains. A swath was cut along the border in the early 1900's. Portions of it are still cleared through the wilderness by the International Boundary Commission.

While we were there at the border, we saw a bald eagle. It proved to be a good sign, for someone saw at least one bald eagle every day while we were in Alaska.

Between Beaver Creek, Yukon, and Tok, Alaska, are lots of ponds, lakes, rivers, and bogs. Each of those had a few ducks with ducklings or a pair or two of trumpeter swans swimming in it.

Black spruce with their stunted size and crooked shapes are plentiful. Their trunks are dark, spindly, and rough. The branches are very short and dark olive green, like tufts of needles sticking out. Many of the trees are dead, killed by spruce beetles.

Ball shaped tangles of twigs and needles close to the trunks are called Witch's Broom and are caused by a fungus. The hardy black spruce grows in poorly drained soil where white spruce will not survive.

Martha's notes said there would be a sled dog exhibition tonight at the Burnt Paw; but when Marvin inquired about it, they said the exhibition hadn't been done for over five years. This gave everyone some extra time so we invaded the nearby campground to use the laundry facilities. There were several buildings with washers and dryers so quite a few of us got much needed laundry done.

Dinner was at Fast Eddy's right beside the motel. Some of us ordered takeout and ate at a picnic table outside the laundry room. We four girls and the four Miler boys had little cabins to stay in instead of rooms in the main building of the motel. That was pretty cool. We had a picnic table outside, and when some of the other girls came by, we made use of it to play games and talk.

We are in Tok, Alaska. We had driven out of rain this morning and had sunshine and warm weather the rest of the day. We are now in Alaska Time Zone, four hours behind the folks at home.

Mileage for today is 289.

TUESDAY, JULY 23

Jealousy is when you count someone else's blessing instead of your own.

We drove from Tok to Valdez to have a cruise on Prince William Sound. We followed the Tok Cutoff southwest to the Richardson Highway then traveled south. To our right were Mt. Kimball and the Chistochina Glacier. To our left were the snowy Wrangell Mountains. We got a good look at Mt. Sanford, one of Alaska's ten highest peaks.

Lunch was soup and sandwiches at Ernesto's in Glennallen. After lunch as we traveled on south, we lost the sun to clouds, mist and fog. We also got stuck in one construction zone after another. The road was rugged and bumpy, giving those in the backseats a shaking up.

Because of the construction, we were running late for our cruise. We were in such a remote area that Martha couldn't call the captain until we got closer to Valdez. When Martha finally talked with the captain, he said that whenever we get there, he'll take us out on the sound. We were the only passengers so it didn't matter if we started a bit late.

We set out in the Lu-Lu-Belle in thick fog. We couldn't even see the thick mountains on both sides of us. The farther out we went, the more the fog lifted. It started raining, and it was cold, wet, and windy; but that didn't keep us inside. We wanted to see everything we could!

We bypassed Bligh Reef where the Exxon Valdez sank in March, 1989, spilling more than 11,000,000 gallons of crude oil. The ensuing oil slick covered

1,300 miles of coastline and 11,000 square miles of ocean, killing thousands of seabirds, otters, whales, seals, and other sea life.

On our way to Glacier Island to see puffins, we passed a sea lion eating a salmon. It surfaced and chewed away at the fish, went back down, surfaced again, and down the hatch went the salmon. Gulls flocked around ready to snatch up any stray bits.

On Glacier Island we saw a few puffins. They nest in niches in the sheer, rock walls; and if you didn't know what to look for, you would never spot them, The captain had to put the bow of the boat right up into an opening in the sea wall before we could see them. One of the puffins was uneasy enough that it flew out and circled behind us until we left.

On the small rocky beaches were Stellar's Sea Lions by the dozens. Big ones, little ones, and in-between, all were barking and grunting and moving lazily around, and making such a racket that I'm sure they couldn't hear each other. Occasionally one would tip off its rocky perch and go for a short swim.

Destination 2 was Columbia Bay to see the Columbia Glacier. It was awesome. Up the bay we went, noticing the temperature dropping down to freezing, the rain stopping, and the wind picking up. All unexpectedly we glimpsed an iceberg, a tiny one, floating out to sea. Now another, and another. On we went with the ice chunks getting more and more numerous. Sea otters and sea lions played around the ice.

Most of the ice chunks were pale, icy blue which was very pretty. Some of the chunks had ice frozen in layers then the chunk had fallen off and splashed sideways into the water. Other chunks were smudged in varying shades of dark gray, brown, and black. The dark color comes from the glacier grinding away at the rocky bottom as it moves along. The rocks are pulverized and the silt ground into the ice, making it black.

Being part of the Pacific, Prince William Sound is salt water and never freezes. The ice chunks, however, freeze to each other as they float. As we went through, the ice layer crackled and popped as it shifted and broke to let us advance. Captain Fred had to slow way down because finally we were completely surrounded by a sea of ice, a sea that was transparent white and blue, shining even in the mist. Ever so slowly the boat would nudge its way between the chunks of ice. The ice would give way but always there was more ice ahead, behind, and beside us. Awesome!

Columbia is a tidewater glacier coming right down the slope to the water's edge. Icebergs are constantly falling off into the water. We went as close to it as we could; then slowly turned around and crept our way back out of the ice surrounding us. The fog and mist lifted, giving us a better view of the sound.

Once we were away from all the ice, the temperature had warmed up about twenty degrees.

On open water headed back to Valdez, the captain turned the wheel over to the passengers for awhile. The night had closed in. It was well after dark when we got back to the harbor.

The closer we got to Valdez, the foggier it became. Fred was going to show us the terminus of the Alaska Pipeline, but it was lost in the foggy darkness.

Although it was 12:15 when we got off at the dock, none of us would have wanted to miss this cruise. It was much better than a few hours of sleep!

At one point we went over the underwater terminal moraine. The moraine is where the face of the glacier was in 1979. That spot is eleven miles from where the glacier face now is. The reason it retreated? In 1977 a large chunk of ice fell off the face leaving a huge crevice in the glacier. Water rushed into the crevice creating more underwater ice which melts faster than ice above the water. Since the waters of the sound don't freeze, the glacier has been melting faster than it could grow in wintertime. The glacier is retreating because more of it is under water and melting. More of it is under water because of the crevice from when the ice chunk fell off.

What caused the crevice? A 4-minute 9.2 earthquake north of the sound that destroyed Valdez in March 1964. Anchorage and Seward both suffered major damage from the earthquake as well. Seems to me that could damage a glacier too. It might be destructive for the glacier and its surroundings, but it is nature following its God ordained path, even by an earth shattering quake.

Bird list for the cruise from what Delbert and I could identify: gulls, arctic terns, cormorants, loons, pigeon guillemots, horned puffins, and bald eagles. There were some little black birds flying low over the water, but with the fog we couldn't figure out what kind they were.

Miles for today from Tok to Valdez were 264.

Be thankful for the troubles that you don't have.

We started off going north on the Richardson Highway on our way from Valdez to Anchorage.

In Keystone Canyon we stopped at the Horsetail Falls and again at Bridal Veil Falls. Horsetail Falls come straight down the canyon walls in narrow streamers. Bridal Veil Falls start out narrow then spread out on both sides as it cascades down the rocky cliff. Both are visible from the road as are several others.

Thompson Pass wasn't as foggy this morning. We could see the glaciers way up top, the green valley down below, and even some of the peaks stretching their heads above the clouds. The pass is beautiful but rugged. Nothing very large grows there. Small shrubs are the largest plants, but it is a lovely green regardless. From the road we could see the Worthington Glacier It comes down between the high peaks, over ridges, across valleys, and over ridges again. It has fingers spread out in all directions going down the slopes.

North of the canyon, before we reached the pass, we were above a ridge to the left. It was green and seamed and ribbed with gullies and gorges. Waterfalls and streams flowed down every slope and crack in the rock.

Here and there we glimpsed the Alaska Pipeline where it runs above ground. It is high enough that wildlife can go through beneath it.

In Matanuska State Park we stopped for a look at Matanuska Glacier. It is about four miles long and two miles wide.

In Palmer, we had a tour of a musk ox farm. A short walk took us to where the little woolly calves played beside the mothers. All the adults seemed rather lazy in the warm sunshine. A set of musk ox horns and some raw wool were in a box beside the trail. We took turns feeling the wool, which was very soft, and holding up the horns which were quite heavier than they looked.

Back on the bus, it must be that someone was bored this afternoon. Maybe he thought everyone else was bored. Whatever the case, a wiggly, squishy, four inch rubber spider started showing up in rather odd places. It especially like to harass someone who was visiting Dreamland. In no time at all the boys were off into bursts of laughter, waking everyone else up.

We went past a side road with a rather unique roadblock. It had huge boulders sitting side by side across the width of the road. In front was a sign saying that the road was closed.

We checked in at our hotel then had some time to spare before our dinner reservation at The Peanut Farm Restaurant. At the restaurant we were in the back room all by ourselves. We split up into tables of two, four, or six.

First we were served a tossed salad. Then we had a main course of corn fritters with honey butter, delicious cod fillets, and several strips of steak with a tasty sauce. Dessert was a three layer, yellow cake with rhubarb and cream cheese fillings. Most of us were curious about the peanut part of the restaurant's name, but we didn't find out what it meant.

In July, Anchorage has almost 18½ hours of daylight compared to January when it has only 6½ hours of light. After dinner we shopped at the nearby Alaska Wildberry Products store. Even when we got done there, it was still daylight.

We had 303 Miles for today.

THURSDAY, JULY 25

Why wish upon a star when you can pray to the One who created it?

Today found us making our way to Homer. Turnagain Arm off Cook Inlet was at low tide. All we saw were tidal flats and wet sand. The arm is bordered by mountains on both sides. The peaks were lost in the clouds although the sun peeked out now and than.

Two eagles were on the sand, and lots of gulls were on the rocky outcrops and in the air.

Farther out there was more water, choppy and restive, and shorelines of green marsh grass about a foot high. The third eagle of the day was flying above the grass.

We found that Jonas Emma did her laundry at 12:15 last night. She said that she jumped out of bed and went to do her laundry in her nightgown. She'd decided that midnight would be a good time to do it because no one else would be awake. She got quite a ribbing about it today though.

At Alyeska Ski Resort we had a tram ride up the mountain. We girls went up a little farther then came back down. We lallygagged around enough that several of us almost missed our ride back down. Martha was motioning for us to start hiking down the mountain trails. Fortunately for us they stopped the tram and opened the doors again for us to get in.

The view from the top of the mountain was priceless. A helicopter was flying below us. The Kenai Mountains are pretty, all covered in green velvet: dirty brown and worn smooth at the tops, short, yellow-green grass on the slopes, brighter green shrubbery farther down surrounding patches of dark green conifers. Little lakes were sprinkled here and there.

From the top the boys had spotted two moose in one of the lakes. We girls tried to find them, but I think we were looking at the wrong lake. We saw them from the tram on the way down though. It was a cow and her youngster.

Moose! A young bull beside the road. He had to get down on his front knees to get a drink from the mud puddle.

Driving along the shore of Cook Inlet, we could see the dim, pale blue, snowy peaks of the mountains on the west side of the inlet. The water was silver blue with slate shadows as the waves played back and forth in the sunshine.

Marvin drove through the small Russian village of Ninilchik. It had a small church, a tiny greenhouse, and a little gift shop. Most of the other buildings were houses, some vacant looking and all wooden and dilapidated. All the yards were weedy and overgrown. We didn't stop, but it would have been interesting to talk with the villagers.

The people in this village are from Russian Orthodox Old Believers. They lived peacefully in Siberia until they were forced out by the Communist Revolution. They moved to China; then in 1949 they scattered around the world. One group ended up here in Alaska. Their four to five hour church services are still held in the traditional Slavonic language.

Deep Creek Beach State Park was on Martha's notes for spotting eagles. We didn't see any eagles but were quite surprised with something just as interesting. When we got there, we discovered that the fishing charters were coming in after a day on the water.

Two log skidders, each manned by a driver and a hook-up person, were zipping up and down the beach. The office person in a little shack told the skidder driver which boat was coming in next. The skidder was hooked up to the right trailer and backed it into the water at an angle. The charters came charging in, barely slowing down to get on the trailers. Before the boat was entirely on the trailer, the skidder moved out of the water, pausing for a few moments to let the hook-up guy get the boat fastened. Up the rise they zipped, parked the trailer, buzzed over to the shack to find out who was coming in next, then headed for the row of trailers to hook up the right one and back it into the water.

We must have watched more than a dozen boats being landed in the short time we were there. It was pretty cool. There are no docks so the passengers had to get off the boats via stepladders.

The boys did see a few eagles up on the hills behind the beach; and right after we got back on the road, we saw a pair of eagles in a tree beside the road.

We got to the Homer Spit, a 4.5 mile long strip of sand and gravel stretching out into Kachemak Bay, in time for the fishermen to get their licenses, explore a bit and eat dinner.

Several of us girls walked the beach on the west side. A sea otter was playing in the waves, gulls were crying and wheeling. There was a big dead sea lion on the beach north of the boardwalk. One big building was up on a humongous piles. The piles, anywhere from eighteen to twenty four inches in diameter, were tall enough that we could walk beneath the building. In the center a swing hung from the beams. It was peaceful swinging slowly, watching the birds, and listening to the endless rush and roar and splash of the wavers.

On the east side of the spit is the harbor. The fish cleaning shacks were busy cutting up the day's catch of Halibut. Believe me, it did not take them long to get one done!

We drove 240 miles today.

FRIDAY, JULY 26

**Fishing and life are similar;
you never know what you have at the end of the line.**

We woke up to pouring rain. At breakfast they said the rain should stop before noon and the boat ride (for the ones who didn't go fishing) was delayed until 12:30.

Moses and Amy, Fannie, and all ten of us girls had the first boat ride. Sam Beachy, the owner of the boat, and his friend first took us to Gull Island. There were thousands of birds flying around, sitting on the rocks, and resting at their nests. Some were swimming and others were diving for their dinner.

The island is an outcrop of rocks jutting up from the waters of Kachemak bay. It was covered with screaming, crying, squawking birds; common murres, pigeon guillemots, herring and glaucous winged gulls, pelagic cormorants, and a few horned and tufted puffins.

On the far side of the island we could see baby gulls in the nests. They were fuzzy gray and just starting to fledge their wing feathers. What a noisy lot! Up close to the rocks it was so loud that we couldn't hear each other talk. Sam said that eagles sometimes come out to the island, making the gulls scatter in all directions. The eagles are skillful enough to catch the gulls in mid air to take them to their nests on shore.

Sea otters were all over the bay, and we saw a few loons too. The weather was still chilly, misty, and overcast. A stiff breeze was blowing, making the water a bit choppy. Mountains surround the bay on three sides like watchful guardians.

After Gull Island, Sam took us to Halibut Cove, a peaceful, tucked in summer vacation community. The cove was very calm with a backdrop of forested mountain slopes coming right down to the water. The shoreline was marked with dry rusty orange seaweed washed up at the high tide line. The only way to get to Halibut Cove is by float-plane or boat so no one lives there in winter.

Sam showed us his vacation cabin on the cove. It was up on tall stilts built almost right into the mountainside. Below it is his boathouse and dock with steps leading up to the cabin.

The channel around an island was impassable. It was low tide and a three foot high sandbar was blocking our way. Sometimes the bar is six feet out of water, and at high tide enough water would cover the bar for boats to sail the channel.

We went around the island on the bay side to get to the east end of the cove. A few oyster farms were there. All the oyster baskets have blue buoys. The workers have to raise the baskets, wash off the oysters, harvest the good ones, then put the baskets back down in the water. If the oysters aren't washed regularly, they'll be covered with barnacles which makes them unsaleable. The workers stay on boats close to the farms while they are taking care of the oysters.

After we came, back to the spit, we convinced Marvin that he should go with the second boatload. We told him we girls can take care of ourselves so on he jumped, telling us to meet at the bus at 5:30.

The other girls wanted to shop after eating so Malinda and I explored the beach both ways. It was quite interesting. There is one road down through the spit with sidewalks on both sides. Shops and restaurants line the street. To the est is the harbor with its fish cleaning shacks and boats. To the west is the beach, and north of all the shops were small tents set up on the sand. I guess some enjoyed camping at the spit.

We discovered some of the others were watching the boats move in and out of the harbor so we joined them after getting an ice cream cone. We thought surely the fishermen would come back soon. At 5:30 Marvin said the charter should be in port within half an hour. Some of us chose to stay and wait for them while others chose to go back to the hotel. Finally they came in, everyone having caught their limit of two halibut except Delbert. He had caught three small ones and kept one. Then he got sick after noon and quit fishing. We didn't get to see the fish because they were cleaned up on the way in.

The fishermen were ready to go by 6:00 am. Once on the boat they were told to settle in because it would be a long ride out to where the halibut are. It was pouring when they started out, but the it had stopped by the time they had reached the first fishing spot. By then it was two hours later and fifty miles out in the Gulf of Alaska.

Since this was such a large charter boat, all twenty men could fish at the same time. The captain ran the boat, and two mates baited the lines with fish. The bait fish were seven inches long and put on the hook whole or cut in half. The sinkers on the lines were three pound weights of lead. The mates took the halibut off the hooks and even helped to reel them in if it was needed. It was a challenge to reel in a halibut. Irvin was the only one that could hold the rod with one hand and reel in with the other.

Altogether, they fished in three different spots. At the first spot they caught a few funny looking red fish that the mates threw back. The captain had told them that he likes to try this spot first when he has an all day charter; there aren't as many halibut, but they usually are much bigger. They fished two hundred feet deep. No halibut.

Then they moved in closer to land and fished at one hundred feet deep Here they caught a number of halibut and some seasickness. Dan was feeling sorry for David who was throwing up. Checking up on David a few minutes later, Dan saw him cranking in a halibut and decide he must not be too sick.

At the third spot the water was considerably rougher. They caught more halibut. Emma was the last one to catch the second keeper. She had caught seven but kept throwing them back because she wanted a bigger one. She was getting a hard time from all the guys who were ready to head to shore. Finally she gave in and kept the next halibut she caught.

They were each allowed two halibut. One had to be less than 28 inches, the other more. Daniel had the biggest one, at 37 inches. They were also allowed to fish for salmon and did catch some. A few disgruntled, ready-to-go-back fishermen thought that Emma caught most of the salmon while trying to catch her BIG halibut.

When the mates were cleaning the fish on the way in, they threw the carcasses in the water. The gulls were right there to grab and eat the fish scraps as fast as they were thrown in.

Even with tangles and bait eaten off the hooks, everyone enjoyed the fishing. They saw another sea lion colony plus some humpbacked whales and a few killer whales. The humpbacks came way up out of the water before diving back under. I guess the fishing was quite tiring through, because naps in the cabin were prevalent on the way back to the harbor.

Back on the spit the fishers were given time to eat then we all found the bus to go back to the hotel. Marvin put 40 miles on the bus just shuttling back and forth between town and the spit today.

On our return to the hotel we stopped at the freezer place. All those who fished went in to give their addresses of where to ship the fish. Altogether they caught 204 pounds of fillets. Everyone thought that was a fair enough catch.

CORN PALACE, SOUTH DAKOTA

BAD LANDS, SOUTH DAKOTA

MOUNT RUSHMORE, SOUTH DAKOTA

SIMON & ESTA MILLER, ST IGNATIUS, MONTANA

KOOTENAI BRIDGE, REXFORD, MONTANA

BRITISH COLUMBIA WELCOME SIGN

BANFF, BRITISH COLUMBIA

BANFF, BRITISH COLUMBIA

LAKE LOUISE

BOW LAKE

COLUMBIA ICEFIELDS

ALASKA HIGHWAY

ATHABASCA FALLS

BLACK BEAR WITH CUB

BEGINNING OF ALASKA HIGHWAY, DAWSON CREEK, BRITISH COLUMBIA

ALASKA HIGHWAY WITH FIREWEED

SUMMIT LAKE

ALASKA HIGHWAY

STONE SHEEP

ALASKA HIGHWAY

CARIBOU

MUNCHO LAKE

BUFFALO ON ALASKA HIGHWAY

HERD OF BUFFALO

YUKON SIGN

ALASKA HIGHWAY

BLACK BEAR

KLUANE LAKE

ALASKA WELCOME SIGN

FAST EDDY'S, WE ATE AND SLEPT HERE

ROAD CONSTRUCTION

ROAD SIGN

VALDEZ

VALDEZ

ICEBERGS

ICEBERGS

LU-LU-BELLE, GLACIER TOUR BOAT THAT SOME OF US DROVE!

THOMPSON PASS

ALASKA HIGHWAY AND OUR BUS

PALMER, ALASKA

ALASKA PIPELINE WITH MARTHA

PALMER, ALASKA

ALYESKA TRAM

MOOSE

HOMER, ALASKA

HOMER, ALASKA

THE CHARTER FISHING BOAT THAT TOOK US HALIBUT FISHING

KACHEMAK BAY

SLED DOGS

PICNIC LUNCH IN ANCHORAGE PARK

DENALI PARK ROAD

GRIZZLY BEARS

CARIBOU SEEN FROM OUR BUS

ALASKAN SALMON BAKE

DENALI NATIONAL PARK

MARVIN PANNING FOR GOLD & END OF ALASKA HIGHWAY

MT MCKINLEY (DENALI)

DALL SHEEP

DALL SHEEP

SIGN FOREST WHERE SOME OF US ADDED OUR OWN SIGNS

MUNCHO LAKE

ROADSIDE RESTROOM ON THE ALASKA HIGHWAY

HUTTERITE COLONY

HUTTERITE KITCHEN

When you complete a puzzle, you know you have made all the right choices.

On our way from Homer to Seward we stopped at Dreamer's Woods, a chainsaw woodcarver's shop. There were all sorts of carvings of all sizes. One was a totem pole with an eagle at the top, then an owl, a bear, a musk ox, another bear, another eagle, and a third bear below that.

The carving in progress was a life sized moose. The carver had worked on it for five days and said two more days should see it finished. He plans to fasten a real rack of antlers to it and has sold it already for $10,000.

We reached Seward early and went to see what the Alaska Sea Life Center had to offer. It is dedicated to the conservation of sea life in and around Alaska. There were sea lions, seals, sea otters, puffins, king eiders, smews, gulls, lots of fishes, and bottom creatures such as starfish, anemones, and urchins. There was a tankful of transparent jellyfish which are always fascinating.

Outside there was a deck looking out over Resurrection Bay. Sometimes they see whales in the bay, but none were there today. The bay is ringed by mountains. It was cloudy and rainy again, so we couldn't see the peaks.

Later in the afternoon we started hiking the trail to the base of Exit Glacier in the Kenai Fiords National Park. The shorter trail was closed off because a mama bear and her two cubs were frequenting the area. The other trail was longer than Marvin had thought so we didn't have time to go all the way to the base. Some of us went as fast and as far as we could.

We reached the out-wash plain below the glacier. The plain was full of rocks and stones that had been carried down the slope by the glacier and left there when it retreated back up the slope. Exit Creek ran and tumbled on its way down across the gravel, stones, and rocks piled wherever the glacier happened to drop them.

The glacier itself could be viewed from the trail before we got to the out-wash plain. Most of our group viewed the glacier from that distance, but it was still awesome! It is considerably narrower at the bottom and has a dark streak running down through its icy blueness. Like all glaciers it is full of cracks and crevices.

Next up was Seavey's Ididaride Dogsled Tours. Mitch Seavey, the owner, is the current record holder for the fastest time to run the Iditarod Race. The oldest person to win it, he has won it three times. One of his sons has also won the race.

Some history of the race: The original Iditarod Trail was created when gold was discovered near the city of Iditarod. Miners carried their gold along the trail by dogsled from Iditarod to Seward. At Seward the gold was put on ships bound for an assayer's office in California.

The race is now run in memory of that first race to save Nome. It also keeps alive the tradition of travel by dogsled through the winter in the north.

The race traverses jagged mountains, frozen rivers, dense forests, during snow storms with zero visibility, at temperatures below zero, and through long hours of darkness.

They hitched up the dogs in teams of fourteen. The dogs were hooked onto a long cable in pairs, pulling the little roofed wagons that are used for training in summer. The wagon could seat seven; one person could stand with the trainer on a step behind the back seat.

Off we went on a two mile ride. We had to stop a few times to let the dogs cool off because they got so warm while running. It was fascinating to watch the dogs work, knowing when to cut a corner sharp and when to go wide. One of the older ones casually jumped the center cable whenever the need dictated then jumped back to her own spot without breaking stride.

The wagon had a brake that the trainer used when we were going downhill or when we slowed down to stop. There are no reins, just "gee", "haw", "okay guys", and "whoa"!

Such a barking and yipping of dogs though! Unless they were actually running, the dogs kept up a constant racket. After our ride we got to pet the dogs a little. One from our team didn't like strangers so we just petted the others to let them know they had done a good job.

Two litters of pups were in their pens right outside the building. One litter was several months old, voracious teeth and all. They chewed at everything they could get their teeth on. The second litter was about a week old. They were sleepy, contented little chaps that looked as if they would purr if they could when we held them.

Then we met Hugo, a blue-eyed Siberian Husky. He is the star in a movie about sled dogs although he has never worked on a dog team. He became a star simply because most people think of sled dogs as huskies, and huskies as in Siberian Huskies, gray and white, big head, and blue eyes.

Inside the shed were Seavey's trophies, newspaper articles of his victories, and some pictures. A dogsled and musher's outfits were there too. They even have booties for the dogs' feet so they don't get sore and cut by snow and ice. The thick goose down musher's parka covers everything except the eyes and nose.

Just as were leaving Seavey's, we saw a young moose. He ducked back into the woods as we came out of the driveway.

We headed for the hotel and something to eat. At the hotel we found both lobby doors propped wide open to let in the fresh air.

Carolyn and I went to the front desk for something. Jonas and Emma were there also and we got to talking with the two desk clerks. One of the clerks told us that several years ago the lobby doors had been open, and a black bear came wandering into the lobby. The clerk on duty took pictures of it from the safety zone behind the desk. Finally they got a maintenance man to carefully shoo the bear back out the doors. The bear headed for the woods while everyone present gave a big sigh of relief.

The clerk told us that she's glad she hadn't been on duty at the time. "Because," she said, pointing to the wall behind her, "there would have been a new door right there!"

Jonas, Emma, Carolyn, and I took a walk down to the harbor. Most of the boats were deserted although a few were still coming in, refueling, or unloading. There were sailboats, cabin cruisers, catamarans, yachts, gigantic tour boats, almost any kind of watercraft imaginable.

When we got back to our room we found Mae, Marilyn, Esther, and Mary there. They stayed until 11:30, and by that time we had decided to have a dress exchange tomorrow. Mae and I would switch, Carolyn and Esther switched, Malinda and Marilyn switched, and Laura would wear one of Mary's dresses. Mary didn't think anyone else's dress would fit her so she said she would wear one of Esther's coverings instead.

Today's mileage is 190.

SUNDAY, JULY 28

Seek to be worth knowing rather than well know.

A big cruise ship docked early this morning in Seward. Most of us went to the harbor to see it. I think there were seven decks above water. Jonas Jr. estimated 700 windows on one side of the ship alone. Imagine being in a boat so big that all the people in my little hometown could fit in three times over!

We're headed for Denali village today. It must have been low tide at Turnagain Arm because it was one big mudflat again. We could see a low, misty rainbow at the mouth of Turnagain for a long time.

Most of the glacial rivers split up into several streams when they're in a flat, gravelly spot. The water finds the easiest channel through the gravel that it deposits at the flats, each streamlet going its own way. This is called braiding which is a very pleasing term for it. Each day may find the braids flowing through a new channel across the flats.

We had another delicious picnic lunch in Anchorage Park. Soon after leaving Anchorage, we passed a moose crash site. The moose was lying in the opposite lane. The vehicle that collided with the animal was dented up and bashed in.

At Denali South View we tried to decide if it was Mt. Denali that we were seeing or not. We could see the lower slopes, but the peaks were all hidden in the clouds. Marvin found out that Denali is entirely covered in snow; if it's cloudy at all you cannot see it from there. Maybe tomorrow we'll have a better chance of seeing it while we're in Denali National Park.

We arrived at Denali Park Village a bit late and supperless. About a dozen of us met a woman from Germany. She could understand and talk our dialect and declared that we must originate from southern Germany. Her husband had stayed at home because he doesn't like to fly. She was with a tour group also and had to speak English with her fellow travelers since none of them understood German. She declared that we made her feel so much better because she had found someone who spoke her mother tongue.

It was a long twilight again. If it's not cloudy, it never really gets dark. After all, in a few hours the sun will come out again!

Miles for today are 371.

MONDAY, JULY 29

Today we had a 6-hour, 135-mile tour in Denali National Park. Wow! It was very awesome, amazing, and breathtaking.

It was grayish dawn when we left and a light rain was falling. Becky, our driver and guide, told us a little about herself on the way to the park entrance. She and her husband live just outside the park in a little wood-heated cabin with no bathroom and no running water. The cabin does have electricity though.

Because digging a well is expensive and water pipes will freeze, they get their water from the community well two miles away and from a spring closer to home. She said they used to stay at the cabin all year, but now they are snowbirds and spend the winter in Oregon.

She also told us several stories:

Bear Encounter One

Becky had been hiking during her vacation. She was at the campground, had her tent pitched, and was making supper at the campfire enjoying the peace and quiet. Suddenly through the evening stillness came the holler, "Hey! Bear!" Before she could move, the bear crashed through her camp so close she could have scratched its back. It was simply in a hurry to get to the riverbank in its search for berries and roots.

Moose Encounter

At one of the rest areas along the Park Road, a fellow bus driver decided to use the woods instead of waiting her turn for the restrooms. In the woods she heard a twig crack behind her. She turned around and there stood a moose! Out of the woods popped a scared bus driver vowing to never again use the woods for a bathroom!

Bear Encounter Two

A friend of Becky's was on a solitary hike when he came upon a sour tempered grizzly. The man waved his arms above his head and hollered as the bear charged. The man stood his ground and it veered off at the last second. At the second charge the bear clipped the guy on the shoulder, knocking him to the ground, and veered off again. The man curled up in a ball and held still. Knowing it made contact, the bear came back. But the "thing" didn't fight back. The grizzly sniffed and pawed at the guy then walked away, having decided it was nothing dangerous.

Right after entering the park, Becky informed us that it's up to us to spot the wildlife because she has to watch the road. If we spotted anything we were to holler, "Stop!" She said its okay if we stop and it turns out to be nothing. She would stop for bears, rocks, moose, and trees.

The park is all about wildlife, right? According to Becky we had excellent spotters on the bus. She even asked if we would go with her again tomorrow, saying her husband will never believe what all we saw. I think all of us saw enough to be satisfied.

We saw three cow moose in the spruce forest, ten ptarmigan beside the road curiously watching the bus, a few arctic ground squirrels, a couple of snowshoe hares, eleven Dall sheep in several bunches, and around sixty seven caribou here, there, and everywhere! (Becky thought it was as if someone had put them in a shaker and scattered them all over the tundra.) And last but definitely not least, we saw twelve grizzlies. Yes, a dozen of them! Four were cubs and the rest were adults. All of them were feeding on soapberries and blueberries.

The closest caribou we saw was a bull walking down the road ahead of us. We followed his tracks for about two miles. Once we caught up with him, we followed him for another half mile or so. Finally he trotted off into the brush at the side of the road and disappeared.

The closest bears were a sow and two cubs less than fifty yards from the road. That was a huge bonus, having them so close! They were just minding their own business, grubbing about for berries and anything else that looks good to a bear.

At one point quite high up on a slope, we went through an active rock slide zone. We could see where the road had been last summer, six feet farther down the slope. Once spring arrived, they regraded the road and hauled in gravel for the new section higher up the slope. The road is open only from mid-May to mid-September.

Becky said the bus drivers are trained to turn around on the narrow road, even on the steep slopes. She asked us if we wanted a demonstration but we informed her that it's not necessary. We will just take her word for it.

At most places there is room for one bus to pass another. At other places the returning bus has to pull off till the bus going up is through.

The tundra is a pretty place in July. Framed by rugged mountains, it has many shades of green, yellow, and brown. Some of the shrubs were just starting to turn red. It has twenty kinds of moss growing on it, giving it a soft, spongy carpet.

Trees are sparse in the tundra although there are lots of shrubs and bushes. The seeming flatness of the tundra is deceiving. The shrubs may grow tall enough for a caribou to hide out in the open where there are no trees.

Looking out over the valleys, we could see the dark green of shrubs in the bottoms, where chalky brown rivers snaked through. Farther up, the mountains were covered in short, yellow-green vegetation or bare brown rocks.

It was cloudy enough that we never glimpsed the snowy Alaska Range so we didn't get to meet Mt. Denali, the highest mountain in North America. It is only two hundred miles south of the Arctic Circle. Record temperatures on the mountain may be 60 degrees below zero. And wind speeds can be up to 100 miles per hour with wind chills of 100 degrees below zero.

After the park we went on north to Fairbanks. We had dinner at the Alaskan Salmonbake. Everything was set up outdoors. There was a big open area where the food was set out, and tables for the dinner guests were scattered here and there among the trees.

There was a salad bar with dinner rolls, baked beans, and macaroni and cheese for sides. Then there was roast beef, beer battered cod, hot dogs, and grilled salmon. Dessert was brownies, lemon bars, mocha parfait, cake, and blueberry and strawberry-rhubarb compote.

There is a pioneer village set up around the salmon bake. It even has a train chugging around giving rides. Some ancient pieces of farming and mining equipment are displayed as well.

TUESDAY, JULY 30

A ship is always safe at shore, but that's not what it was built for.

Today is our last full day in Alaska. In a week and a half we'll be at home again. Where did all the time go?

This morning we had a ride on the Chena River on the Riverboat Discovery III. It was an A rated tour with the theme being how the people, past and present, live in the interior of Alaska, away from the coast, and without a lot of roads. It was interesting and made me wonder if I would be to content to live like they do.

Not far down the river we watched a pilot take off and land on the river in his floatplane. The plane was built in 1951 and ran like a charm. In winter the pilot puts skis on the plane instead of the floats so he can still use the river for his runway. The river is generally frozen over from mid-October to mid-April. Besides planes, cars and trucks are driven on the frozen river along with snowmobiles and dogsleds. Even people on skis travel the river in winter.

Our next stop was to watch a dogtrainer work with sled dogs and pups in training. The trainer was the daughter of Susan Butcher, a winner of the Iditarod Race. We watched her do a test run with the dogs pulling a gutted four wheeler. It looked kooky, but the dogs had a blast at it.

When they were done with their run, the trainer let them cool off in the river. They splashed and played merrily.

We turned around where the Chena meets the Tanana River. Both rivers looked murky and sluggish right there. The banks were lined with trees, mostly fir and spruce. Farther back were the low forested mountains. The water was fairly calm and ducks were all over.

On the way back we stopped at Chena Village. There we had a taste of how the Athabascan people lived. Ancient canoes were made of birch bark, a naturally water resistant material, stretched over bent spruce wood frames. Canoes were used to travel during the summer.

They hunted caribou during spring and fall migrations, and moose year round. Traplines were run in winter, and rivers were fished during the salmon runs in summer.

Because of this varied food supply, they had to have a nomadic life just to survive. Their homes, moved eight or nine times a year, were made from bent spruce branches tied with rawhide strips and covered with caribou hides. They could be taken apart easily and carried to the new camp spot. In the winter they traveled with snowshoes made from birch or spruce wood and rawhide strips

After contact with trappers, missionaries, hunters, and miners from the east, their way of life changed dramatically. Winter homes were log cabins chinked with moss, animal fat, and moose hair. The roofs were made of logs lined with birch bark. More logs edged the roof, then soil was put on to fill the roof to the brim. Grass seeds were planted on the roof. The bark kept the roof waterproof against rain and melting snow. The soil insulated it and the grass bound everything together.

Along the trapline the Athabascan would build tiny line cabins a day's journey apart. Now he could have a much longer trapline and would not have to come home every evening for shelter. The Athabascans built a cache wherever it was needed to store their furs and meat out of reach of wild animals.

Any hides they had were used for clothing or bedding. Beds were made from spruce branches and caribou hides.

Fur parkas were made from caribou and trimmed with beaver and wolf.

The hoods were made from wolverine and wolf skins. Wolverine fur has an oil that keeps your breath from sticking to the fur and then freezing, so that was put closest to the face to prevent frostbite. Wolf skin was used on the outer edge.

Two skins of each animal were needed for one hood. The wolf skins were not worked with much so they were still stiff. A wind from behind would blow up and over the hood, creating a warmer pocket of air for the face. In an oncoming wind the hood was pulled forward more tightly, making just a small hole for air to get in to the face.

Wolverines were prized for meat and fur partly because they were so hard to catch. Foxes were also caught. Silver, red, and gray could all be from the same litter. Ermine were trapped, and of course timber wolves were too. Hanging from one of the caches in the village was a wolf hide measuring 73 inches from the tip of the nose to the tip of the tail.

A baby carrier was made of wood and rawhide strips. Mothers would line the bottom with soft moss and grasses. When the baby soiled it, the mother would replace it with clean moss.

At the fish camp were two small A-framed tents covered with spruce branches and outfitted with spruce and caribou beds. A fishwheel was turning in the river's current. On the bank was a fish-drying rack.

We were shown how the Indians filleted their salmon leaving the two fillets connected at the tail. The flesh was scored into strips crosswise to dry more efficiently. Then the fillets were hung on the rack with the meat side out. After drying in the sun for a few days, the salmon were moved to the smokehouse.

In the center of the smokehouse was the firebox. After a batch of fish was smoked directly over the fire, it was moved farther away, making room for a new batch over the fire.

The chum salmon was dog food so they were dried thoroughly and smoked with spruce or driftwood or any trash wood. The king salmon was food for the people. They were also dried and smoked but were not as hard as the dog food. Alder or birch was used to smoke the king salmon.

When our time was up at Chena Village, we went back to the Discovery Hall dining room for dinner. Tables for twenty were set up with the chinaware all ready. There were several hundred people aboard the riverboat and there was room for everyone to sit down and eat.

Pitchers of water and iced tea were ready to be poured into pint jar shaped glasses. Miner's stew, made of tender beef, mushrooms, and potatoes was served in small cast iron kettles. Roasted veggies were also served in the kettles. Dinner rolls, salad and a German chocolate bar completed the meal.

At the Discovery Hall there is a room with a temperature of 40 below zero. It's a small room kept at this temperature for tourists to experience how cold it gets in the winter in interior Alaska. Quite a few of us tried it. It wasn't all that bad because there was no wind in the room.

After dinner we had a short train ride through the Goldstream Valley to Gold Dredge 8. The cars on the train were open with a roof but no windows. The narrator told us the story of how gold was mined in the valley.

Drift miners first found and mined gold outside Fairbanks. They dug a shaft to bedrock them followed the drifts of ore underground. Next came the placer miners who panned for gold in the gravel of the creek bottoms and riverbeds.

FE, Fairbanks Excavation Company, decided it would be worth their while to dig for gold in the valley. They had a dredge built in California then taken apart again and put on railcars bound for a port city. There the parts were loaded onto a boat and shipped to Valdez. At Valdez the parts were again loaded onto railcars, 115 of them, and taken to the mine in Fox outside Fairbanks. There at the mine the dredge was reassembled.

The process of dredge mining is extremely detrimental to the landscape. The first one hundred fifty feet of topsoil was washed away using water, from the Davidson Ditch that the company had dug. Then they devised a way to thaw the frozen bedrock by driving pipes into the ground. Water was run through the pipes to an exit hole in the point. As the water trickled out of the point, it thawed the surrounding area up to three feet away.

Dynamite was used to loosen the bedrock. The dredge dug up the blasted pieces, ran them through, and found the gold. The tailings were left behind in a mess. The gold was formed into bricks and sent to California.

Finally the price of gold wasn't high enough for the company to continue mining. Although dredge mining was discontinued, placer mining still goes on in the Goldstream Valley.

Our train stopped at the dredge. Beyond the dredge was a huge pavilion with rows of long water troughs. Benches were set on both sides of the troughs and gold pans were laid out ready for us.

Each of us were given a poke of pay dirt and directions on how to pan for gold properly. Pour the dirt into the pan, get some water in the pan, tilt it, and swirl the water around. Then tilt the pan at a steep angle to wash away the top layer of dirt and gravel.

Gold is heavier than water so it will settle to the bottom of the pan. So keep on swirling, tilting, and washing until there's only a tablespoon of very fine sand left in your pan. Swirl the water in your pan carefully to separate the sand from the gold then dump out the water. Each flake of gold could be picked up by touching it with a dry fingertip. We had little black containers to put the flakes into.

In the giftshop the gold is weighed and valued. If you wish, you can have the gold put into a charm, keychain, bookmark, or some such trinket to display it. The average find is ten to twelve dollars worth. The most for anyone on the bus was $27 for Marvin.

After panning for gold, we wandered around the giftshop and explored the dredge. There was a 19 ounce nugget. It is the twenty fifth largest nugget ever found in Alaska's gold fields and is worth $75,000. The dredge itself is very fascinating. It is three stories high with belts, conveyors, and screens still left intact.

We rode the train back to where we began and had a short course of history on the Alaska Pipeline. For years we have heard about the pipeline and now we saw it up close!

Twenty thousand workers worked twelve hours a day, seven days a week for three years to complete the pipeline at a cost of $8 billion. The pipeline is eight hundred miles long, half of it above ground. And carries an average of 1.8 million barrels of oil a day to the Valdez terminal. The company discovered an underground pipe is impractical in permafrost. The hot oil thawed the ground turning everything into a soft, muddy mess. So in areas of permafrost, the pipe is above ground, insulated, and built in a zigzag to allow for contracting and expanding in severe temperatures. The oil itself stays hot enough on its eight hundred mile journey that it doesn't freeze. The pipe is not securely fastened to its supports so it can move back and forth in an earthquake, hopefully avoiding damage to the pipe. Wherever it is built above the ground, it is high enough for wildlife to pass by beneath it.

The oil is from 120 to 140 degrees while running through the pipe. It cools a little as it runs, forming petroleum jelly and paraffin against the walls of the pipe. To clean the pipe they send a pipe pig through. A pipe pig is a huge cone shaped scraper that cleans the pipe as it travels with the flow of oil. At Valdez the pigs are cleaned and trucked back to Prudhoe Bay to be used again.

Since the waters of Prince Williams Sound don't freeze over, the Valdez terminal is the northernmost ice-free port in America. Because of this, oil can be loaded onto tankers at Valdez year round.

Tomorrow is our last day in Alaska. I think I could stay up here for another month and not get homesick.

WEDNESDAY, JULY 31

Happiness is a way of travel not a destination.

This morning we all wished Roy a safe flight home. He has back problems and decided to fly home from Fairbanks instead of riding the bus another week and a half.

Our first stop was the Santa Claus House in North Pole, Alaska. It is a store with all kinds of Christmas decorations and gift items. Mail may be dropped off here also to be postmarked as coming from the North Pole.

As we passed Eielson Air Force Base, we saw about a dozen military planes take off and land in formation. Those pilots certainly have a lot of skill! I wouldn't want to fly so close to another plane.

The Knotty Shop was next specializing in things made from spruce burls. There were benches, planters, little chests, and knickknacks.

Arsenic occurs naturally in the soil this far north. The burls are growths on the spruce trees stemming from all the acid in the soil.

On the road we spotted another moose. Emma hollered out and woke everyone that had been sleeping. As the bus slowed down, the moose ducked back into the woods. Marvin decided not to back up since it had disappeared, and we went on our way to the tune of Emma's parting shot: "You'd better have horns by the time we see you again!"

We continued traveling southwest of Fairbanks. Some time before noon we noticed the sky had cleared and the sun was shining. To the west we could now see the glorious snow-covered Alaska Range. Was it Mt. Denali we were seeing? Could it be?

Yes, it could! At Delta Junction, Marvin stopped at the Visitor Center. He asked the woman if that's Mt. Denali that we see. She answered yes; that other travelers had been dropping in and asking about it too.

Imagine it! Only 30% of summer visitors get to see the peak of Denali. On our last day in Alaska we became part of that 30%. The grand snow white peak jutted up into the blue sky. It was imposing even from a distance of almost two hundred miles. What a day brightener! It was definitely one of the most beautiful sights on the trip.

We watched it as long as we could, losing it as it faded from sight in the blue distance. It seemed as if we were granted one last gift from Alaska: a view of the North's pride and joy, its majestic guardian.

Lunch was at Fast Eddie's in Tok. After eating, we continued east and south on the Alaska Highway. To our right snowy mountains stretched out as far as we could see. Somewhere in all those mountains is Mt. Logan, the highest peak in Canada.

We crossed the border into Canada and stopped at customs around 3:30. When we continued on our way, we had the highway to ourselves most of the afternoon. A few of us saw a porcupine. Other than that we didn't see much wildlife, just awesome wilderness displaying the fingerprints of our mighty God.

Two hours before sundown, the sky is a clear blue though not as deep blue as we see at home. A few puffy white clouds are drifting along in the golden light of the evening sun. Blue sky, white clouds, golden sunshine lighting up the snowy mountains int he distance, what a pretty picture!

We stopped for the night in Destruction Bay on the western shore of Kluane Lake, the largest lake in the Yukon. Six of us girls decided it would be worth our while to watch the sun set from the lake shore. We headed across the road and down to the lake. At the boat landing we met a guy who was taking pictures. Not wanting to trespass, we asked if this was private property.

"Oh, no!" the man replied. "This is the Yukon!"

Then he asked where we're from so we told him a little about our trip, saying we're returning from Alaska.

Then he asked if we stopped at the Kluane Museum. When we told him we had, he said his mother runs the museum.

We girls crawled over the large rocks on the harbor banks. Malinda walked south along the shore while Mae and Laura rock hiked all the way to the end of one embankment. Carolyn and Marilyn sat down to watch the sun slip down under the horizon, and I joined them after wading in the cold shallows.

It was so peaceful. The only noises were ourselves and the water lapping gently on the shore. The sky turned pink, red, and purple in the west as the sun set and the quietness of night settled down.

It was the perfect ending to a good day.

Miles for today were 428.

**Blaming others for your problems is like blaming donuts for being fat;
it wasn't the donuts, it was your choice.**

Sunshine and blue sky for the second day in a row! Martha said she had talked with a lady who said they're enjoying the nice weather. First they had the wildfires, then the rains, and now they're enjoying the beautiful oncoming fall weather. Think of it: fall in early August.

Emma and Fannie switched outfits for today. Emma looked like a Holmes County lady and Fannie looked like A Geauga lady. They had the rest of us laughing at them. I guess they had their share of laughs while trying on each other's dresses. Jonas Jr. remarked that he had to help Emma pull and tug to get Fannie's dress on this morning. He also said that he's not going to let Emma do it ever again!

At the south end of Kluane we halted for a dozen Dall ewes and lambs. They'd come down to the lake for water then started back up the slopes as we neared. Skipping and jumping up and right and left and on up, they followed their well known path to the upper regions. That's when we noticed more of them up there. Altogether we saw about three dozen sheep.

Ground squirrels stood stock still beside the road. Most of them only moved their heads as they watched the bus go by. A few of them got frightened and made a break for safety in the ditch.

A coyote trotted across the road.

At Whitehorse we ate lunch then went to the fishladder to see if the salmon were running this far up the Yukon yet. No such luck. So far only a handful of salmon had reached Whitehorse.

We stopped at Teslin for a half hour break. Fannie sneaked back to the bus and dressed up in a rainsuit, a cap, and a curly red wig, and a weird pair of glasses. When the rest of us returned, she was sitting about halfway back with her head tipped back and eyes shut.

Amid all the laughter one of the boys dripped water on her face. She licked at it but didn't open her eyes or smile

The boys called out, "Marvin, you've got an extra person on board here!"

When Marvin went to Investigate, he asked, "Do you belong on here?"

"No."

"Well, you can go with us for now. We'll see if we can find a piece of cardboard and a corner for you somewhere."

We arrived at Watson Lake with two important things to do: eat dinner and visit the Signpost Forest. Martha remarked about how those last miles for every day just seem to take so much longer. Steve put up his hand and asked if we could do the last miles first tomorrow.

Martha laughed and said she knows how he feels. She's always wanted to find a way to wash dishes first and then eat!

The posts in the signpost forest are set up in rows and sections. They put in new posts every year to accommodate all the signs that summer tourists bring to add to the collection. In 2018 the count of signs was over 88,000.

People used anything as signs: shoes, metal signs, wooden signs, carved boards, plates, frisbees, caps, pie plates, pans, skillets, oars, hubcaps, anything imaginable. Carolyn tried to find her brother's sign, but there's no way to find one particular sign unless you can spend all day.

It all started when a lonely homesick soldier was asked to repair a directional post for the highway. The soldier decided to add a sign for his hometown of Danville, Illinois. From that beginning almost eighty years ago, there is a plethora of signs from all over the world.

We are at Andrea's Hotel, the one with all the loafers outside. We tried to be back from the Signpost Forest before dark because it really wasn't comfortable being outside at all.

Jonas Jr. borrowed Fannie's curly wig, and Joe put on her weird hat and glasses. They went to visit the boys' room. The boys got quite a laugh out of it. You'll have to ask them if they were scared.

Miles for today are 473.

WELCOME TO ALASKA

Got the extra mile; it's never crowded.

A few miles east of Watson Lake we encountered a young gray wolf. He was at the edge of a clearing and studied the stopped bus for awhile before trotting back into the woods. That was a good way to start the day!

By 6:30 we had also seen a heard of 75 buffaloes, a few lone buffaloes, a buck, four hares, two swans, and a young black bear. The bear was curious, popping over the edge of the bank to see what he had heard.

More buffaloes. The count is around 120 so far today.

The boardwalk back to Liard Hot Springs is about half a mile long. There is wetland on both sides of the walk. Several sandpipers were pecking around in the shallow water.

The springs are surrounded by trees. The corner where the hot water bubbles up is blocked off so no one gets burned. Not far away from where the hot water bubbles up, it is joined by cold water from a spring. The water is kept at a constant 110°-120° in the first pool spring and a little cooler in the next one. It did feel good. Most of us just stuck our feet in.

Marvin washed the front end of the bus then joined us at the springs. He started to say it would feel great if we just dove in. Then to our surprise he emptied his pockets and took off his belt. In he went. Afterward on the way to lunch he told us that he had headed a boys' camp for a few years. Anything that he'd wanted the boys to do, he'd had to expect to do first to show them how.

That was why he had jumped in at the hot springs: he was telling everyone else to jump in and then he thought, "Maybe I'd better do it myself."

A couple more loner buffaloes. One was a big bull walking the edge of the road as if the world belonged to him, very unconcerned about traffic.

Another bear on the left. Two adult stone sheep and one lamb.

Lunch was at Northern Rockies Lodge on the shore of Muncho Lake. We had a choice of spaetzle, schnitzel, or vegetable spaetzle. Several days ago we had marked our choices and Martha had called them in so they knew how much of each to prepare.

We arrived early so we walked down to the lake. The water was as cold in the lake as it had been warm at the springs. That didn't stop us girls from dipping our feet in though. The water is picture perfect: deep turquoise blue and very clear. Across the lake the mountains stretch from east to west. They reach 7,000 feet in elevation. The summits are bare gray windswept rock with a few patches of snow still clinging to the north slopes. The lower reaches of the mountains are covered with trees. The lake is right at the foot of the mountains and gives a nice reflection of them.

Lunch was delicious. The spaetzle was like small dumplings served with beef and veggies. The schnitzel was breaded fried pork with veggies and fries. We were the only ones there, fairly filling the dining room.

Not realizing a waitress was right behind him, Harry took a few bites and remarked, "Not bad for a roadkill!"

Everyone close enough to hear, including the waitress, burst out laughing. Later the waitress was in the kitchen talking to the others and all of them had a good laugh about it.

In the dining room of the lodge is a hand carved wood map of the region around Muncho Lake. It shows the lodge and all the cabins they have to rent in the wilderness. Every stream and lake is shown in detail along with the highway passing through.

On the road again we saw a single caribou. Then seven stone sheep. Then a couple more caribou.

At Toad River Lodge we stopped for a break and some ice cream. The walls and ceiling of the store are decked with ball caps. They have a count on the whiteboard of the "world's largest hat collection".

The count for today was 11,231. The front room is all covered so they started using the walls in the back where the restrooms are.

While going through Stone Mountain Park, we saw half a dozen more caribou. West of Summit Lake were twenty seven stone sheep and another black bear. Farther on a double rainbow lit up the sky, and we saw two white tailed deer and some cranes.

At last we arrived in Fort Nelson again at the "jail" hotel. We named it that when we were here before because all the walls were built of cinder blocks, even inside in the halls.

Marvin took eight of us to the laundromat down the street. He had to get fuel for the bus and said he'd stop at the laundromat on his way back in case someone wanted a ride back to the hotel. We finished before he came back so we just walked the half mile.

Steve got the idea of having the hotel van take us to the sports field a mile and a quarter away so we could play volleyball until dark. It took a little time to get everyone rounded, but finally we all piled in. The van had no navigator seat and the back seat had been removed. Sixteen of us crammed in where there was seating for only nine. The driver said she'd take the back road for two reasons: there were fewer stop signs and also fewer RCMP officers on patrol. She told us not to tell her boss how she overloaded the van.

The volleyball courts were sand which made for some interesting belly flop dives. We played more than an hour before a huge bank of clouds told us we should head for the hotel. We had over a mile to walk, and it had started to get dark. Thankfully we made it back before it rained.

Today's mileage was 323.

SATURDAY, AUGUST 3

The only person you should be better than, is the person you were yesterday.
Today our route stretched from Fort Nelson, British Columbia, to Grande Prairie, Alberta. An hour after we started, we saw a doe and two white spotted fawns.

At Sikanni Campground we stopped for a restroom break. All they had was several "adventurous" outhouses that looked as if they hadn't been cleaned in three decades or so. The doors didn't even shut right. Good, clean rest areas are hard to find in Canada; if nothing else, we learned that much on this trip!

In the gas station/store was a sign that said, "There is not a single mosquito in Sikanni. They are all married and have children!"

Yesterday at Toad River I found a magnet and showed it to Carolyn. It had the caption, "Before and after driving the Alaska Highway." A plump Garfield was the before, and the after was a frazzled, electrocuted kitty. Both of us laughed with the same idea: it was perfect for Marvin.

At Sikanni we made sure we were the last ones to leave the bus. I slipped the magnet along with a note Carolyn wrote into Marvin's folder on the dash. After lunch he picked up his folder and the magnet fell out. Martha walked back through the aisle showing it to everyone. Amid the shouts of laughter Marvin found the note. Talk about perfect timing. I never thought hat everyone would be on the bus when he discovered it. He stuck the magnet on the dash for the rest of the trip.

At 2:00 we were back at the beginning of the highway, Dawson Creek. Here is where the road began because this was as far as the railroads went in 1942.

Eli was trying to get into their room tonight when we girls came upon them. The door just wouldn't open, no matter how he swiped the key. Daniel offered to go the desk for a new key. Then Eli looked at the key in his hand. It was a key from the hotel we were in last night. He'd put it in his pocket this morning and forgotten to return it!

Carolyn wanted a foot treatment from Lizzie so she ordered pizza for supper. We four girls joined Ada, Lizzie, and Barbara for supper in their room. Afterward Ada, Lizzie, Carolyn, Laura went shopping. Barbara said she was going to shower and climb into bed. Malinda and I went to see what Esther and Mary were doing and ended up playing a game with them.

Mileage for today is 361.

SUNDAY, AUGUST 4

The life you live is the lesson you teach.

We attended services at the Rosedale Mennonite Church this morning. It was very interesting. We sang a few hymns then four couples went up front to sing. Then we all sang again. One of the men had an opening and a prayer followed by the pastor's sermon which was inspiring. It touched on life, and how God gives us life and everything pertaining to life. What a loving God we have! Another member spoke a few words then we prayed again and sang another hymn. It felt satisfying to be part of a church service again.

The likeness of their service and ours was surprising and pleasant. As Delbert said, hundreds of years ago our ancestors came from the same place. Their people moved to Poland to escaped persecution. From there they migrated to Russia then finally moved to North America. About a hundred years before that the Amish started moving to America directly from Germany.

A scrumptious potluck dinner awaited us after the services. There was too much food to taste it all. Home-cooked food is always delicious when you're traveling!

We had some time to visit and got to know some of the people and how they live. Their hospitality was so warm and inviting and friendly.

After leaving the church, we went to a nearby Hutterite colony. From across the fields you can see the big cluster of buildings that make up the hub of the colony.

We were welcomed by a cheerful old woman on a wheelchair. Then one of their leaders showed us their chicken butchering operation. They put through three thousand chickens every week. The chickens are raised in the colony. The Hutterites butcher them, keep what they need, then sell the rest of them.

Three of the Hutterite girls showed us single girls around the rest of the colony. We visited the kindergarten where the children sang a German song for us. In another room in the same building is where the children take their naps.

A few older women take care of the small children while the school aged children and older boys and girls and parents get the work done.

The dining hall is large enough to accommodate all the grown ups. The men sit on one side of the room, the women on the other. The 6 to 15 year olds eat in a separate room attended by supervisors.

Mothers with children under three go to the kitchen to get something to feed the little ones at home.

The kitchen is huge with every imaginable appliance and giant sized gadget available including an electric bread slicer to slice a whole loaf of bread at once. The bread mixer is about three feet in diameter. One batch of bread makes 35 loaves which will last them a week.

A head cook makes menus for a week at a time then 21 women and girls take turns, three at a time, being cook for a week. From what Joanna, who showed us around, said, if you come from a larger family, your turn to cook comes around more often. She is an only child so her doesn't come around as often. She wishes it would because she likes to cook.

The fruit cellar was filled with rows of jars of canned goods. Most of it was in gallon or half gallon jar. Joanna said it doesn't seem to take long to can all the fruits and vegetables if everyone helps.

The church is a plain white building. In its basement are the schoolrooms. One of the elders teachers the German classes, but they hire someone from outside the community to teach the rest of the lessons.

The laundry has seven or eight commercial size washers and two dryers. The women make their own lye soap then put it into a heated kettle to melt so they can use it for the laundry.

Joanna showed us her home. They have two sewing machines and a serger in the basement besides Joanna's bedroom. She has a bedroom suite that she was given when she turned sixteen. Her boyfriend, who lives in another colony, gave her a keyboard. So far she has learned to play a German wedding song on it.

In this colony everyone gets an allowance every month so there are things a person may have for his own. Joanna and her mother make decorated boxes to sell at a farmer's market, and they may keep the money they earn. Work, food, and money for income and expenses is still communal though.

Grain farming is a big source of income for them. The Hutterites in Alberta are known for buying a tract of poor, rundown farmland and starting a new colony. In a few years the ground is built up, and they are making a profit.

Technology and progress in tools, machinery, and so forth are used to the full. There are no limits to something bigger, better, and more efficient.

We all wished we had more time to visit the colony. Joanna tried to convince us girls to stay for a week and let the others go home without us. She was sure we'd enjoy it.

From the Hutterites we drove to Edmonton. On the way Moses fell asleep with his head back and mouth open. No one noticed until he started to snore then Fannie decided to put something in his mouth. Getting some twizzlers from Emma, Fannie knotted them together.

Meanwhile Moses woke up, guessed what was going on by all the sly grins, and accused someone of having bad intentions.

He dozed off again in a few minutes, this time with his mouth shut. Fannie went back for more twizzlers. Waking up again, Moses spotted them as she came back to her seat. He remarked that he should go sit on the front seat; he was sure he could sleep in peace and safety there.

Later Dan was nodding off. Carolyn begged a string of licorice from Fannie and draped it over his glasses. Waking up, he looked at Carolyn and said, "You look pretty red!" When she just hem-hawed a bit, he warned, "You know I pay my debts with interest. You'd better watch out!"

A long while later Carolyn was so glad that we had only a couple more miles to Edmonton. When I asked why, she said, "Because I don't dare go to sleep with Dan right across the aisle!"

We arrived at the hotel in Edmonton having put on 307 miles today.

MONDAY, AUGUST 5

You live only once. False; you live every day.

For a few hours today we were at the West Edmonton Mall, the world's largest indoor shopping mall. There was fairly good bookstore, a replica of a ship, a water park, a skating rink, and a miniature golf course. Down below there was a sea life exhibit: some sharks, other fish, snakes, lizards, and penguins. Seven of the sharks were over five feet long, all nurse sharks. Two big green sea turtles swimming around also.

In eastern Alberta, landscape is gently rolling, mostly cropland with some forests and little woodlots. Fences, dirt country roads, and few and far between farmsteads make a pleasant picture.

Canola is in bright yellow bloom, hay has been cut, wheat heads are popping out, clear blue lakes are scattered here, there, and everywhere.

This afternoon we played a Do You Know Your Fellow Travelers game. Each of us signed a paper then wrote two true things and one false thing about ourselves. Martha read the three statements, and we guessed who wrote them and which one was false.

For most of them we could tell which was false once we knew who wrote the statements.

Lora's false statement was a good one: "I have to drag Miriam out of bed by her feet every morning." She told us it's the opposite; Miriam is always out of bed first.

Delbert had the prizewinner though, I think. His three statements were:
I do not know how many acres of land I own.
I love my Job.
I have 39 birdhouses put up around the home place.

The third one is true. The first one is also true because the deed and the description for his land don't match. The second one was false because he doesn't love his job; he only likes it.

When we arrived in Saskatoon, our hotel had an adventurous ordeal waiting for us. Martha couldn't vouch for all of us. One person from each room had to show ID before we could get our keys. I'm glad that didn't happen more often.

Some of us decided to try out the go-kart track across the street from the hotel. When Mary, Esther, Carolyn, and I arrived, we joined Jonas Jr., Emma, Daniel, Steve, Samuel, and Wilma as spectators. Aden, James, Lora, Miriam, Marty, Harry, and Irvin were racing around the track.

The track was paved, bumpy, and lined with tires on both sides for bumpers in case anyone's go-kart went out of control. Several street lights lit up the track so you could see whom you crashed into.

Marty, Harry, and Lora were the aggressive ones. We almost split with laughter at their antics. Occasionally someone got stuck at the tires. The carts have no reverse so you had to wait until the owner came around and pulled you loose. Meanwhile everyone else zips around you. The owner got plenty laughs out of it too.

The carts are low with a bumper frame all around and a seatbelt. Helmets were required. Old Honda motors ran the carts which had awesome steering The red pedal was the brake; the green one was the gas. Only one pedal may be pushed at a time. Letting off the pressure on the gas pedal slowed it down enough to round the curves. The brakes weren't really necessary except to avoid crashes.

After some other folks had a turn, Irvin and Harry bought ten rides for whoever wanted one. Esther, Carolyn, Steve, Aden, and I had go-around.

Steve, Carolyn, and I had a three cart crash. The owner came to get us loose and just laughed. It was blast, zipping around the track, trying to cut corners to catch up with the next person, and at the time staying ahead of the person behind you.

Harry, Irvin, Marty, Lora, and Jonas Jr. had the next shift. We others laughed and laughed over Lora. She managed to stay ahead although Harry ran her aground once. Lora decided to fix Harry and Marty by staying in the middle of the track. It wasn't wide enough to pass on either side so they were stuck behind her. When their time was up, Lora did the last half lap at low speed still in the middle with the rest putt putting behind her.

The track guy was enjoying it so much that he gave them extra time. Afterward he told Lora she had done a good job. Lora climbed out of her car, plunked her helmet on the shelf, pumped her fists, and declared, "Champion!"

Emma found a dead bedbug on her pillow. Then she saw a live bug scampering across the floor of their room. It would have been interesting to hear her screech! She taped both bugs to the hotel room key. Out came their mosquito spray. Everything was sprayed including the bed. All their belongings were kept off the floor. Even with all that, Emma didn't sleep until 2:00 am. The next morning they reported the bugs at the front desk and were told it wasn't bedbugs. Emma didn't believe that, though.

Our miles for today are 347.

**A flower doesn't think of competing with the flower next to it;
it just blooms.**

Martha's thought for the day for the go-karters: Never haste to end a day; there are too few of them in a lifetime. That goes well with last night because it was after 10:00 when we got back to the hotel.

We had an hour at the Legislature Building in Regina, Saskatchewan. First we had to pass security and the metal detector then we had a guided tour of the building. We split up into two groups so there wouldn't be so many people for each guide.

In the center of the building is a rotunda open all the way to a skylight under the dome. The skylight is 53 meters above the ground floor. Just in that area of the building are marbles from Italy, Vermont, Norway, and Cyprus. The railing around the rotunda, pillars, and floors are all made of marble. The grand staircase is made of marble from Quebec. The pillars in the center of the building are solid marble, the small ones weighing three tons and the large ones five tons. In all there are thirty four different marbles used in the building.

We sat in the special guest section of the legislature's session room. The room is built in the shape of the Tudor crown with gold plated brass flowers on the ceiling for the gems of the crown. The Premier's seat was directly across from us. To our left and right were seats for the public who attend sessions. To the right of the Premier's seat are the desks of the reigning party, to the left is where the other party sits. Currently the reigning party has 47 seats while the other one has only 13. In the center is a table holding a golden mace in a case. In session the mace has to face the majority party's seats.

All the woodwork was oak: benches, chairs, desks, table, and trim work. Men from England were hired to do all the carving and cut work in the wood.

The library was lined with books of any nature and subject. One part is open to the public; the other room is just for members of the government.

Paintings of Premier's past and present line the walls of one room and the corridor. One end has pictures of the construction of the building which was done in 1908-1912 at a cost of $1,800,000.

When we finished inside, we crossed the street to stroll through the gardens. Marvin had parked the bus at the lower end of the gardens beside the lake. There were wide paths between the blooming flowers. On each side was a row of trees. The view from the upper end was the best with all the colorful flowers leading your eyes down to the calm blue waters down at the other end.

Saskatchewan is fairly flat like eastern Alberta. There are few trees breaking up the prairie, and occasionally we saw an oil well. The highway and railroad run parallel for miles, going southeast of Regina. It looks as if it's been dry here lately.

Our border crossing was uneventful, much better than the last two times although it took an hour to process all the paperwork.

We girls went to Walmart which was not far south of the hotel. While I was waiting for the others, Steve came around. The hotel clerk had told him that if we wanted to play volleyball in the yard by the water tower, we should go ahead and play; no one would chase us off. Steve wanted to see if he could find a volleyball net at Walmart since we only had a ball on the bus no net. He found a net for $7.50. (Does the price tell you anything?)

We rounded up the rest of the single guys and girls except Delbert and headed for the water tower. When Esther, Mary, Malinda, and I got there, Steve and Daniel were setting up the net. It was a plastic affair with plastic tripod poles and a six inch inflatable ball.

We decide to get the real ball off the bus. Esther knew where the ball was, and

I knew where the bus had been so we trotted down the sidewalk back the way we had just come. The bus had been moved meanwhile. Finally we found it beyond Walmart just as far south of the hotel as the tower is north of it. I tried the door and of course, it was locked.

Still puffing from running, I thought a bit then guessed that Marvin and Martha were probably in the nearby Mexican restaurant. When we entered, Marvin gave us a quizzical look then smiled, reaching for his keys when I said we wanted the volleyball. He laughed when I said we have to place to play, and Steve got a net at Walmart, and we're good to go once we have the ball.

We played as long as the twilight lasted. We decided we had a 'genuine' North Dakota volleyball court: cheap plastic poles, cheap net that didn't bounce the ball back out, and a boundary line made of crocs and flip flops. We got more than $7.50 of fun out of it too!

Carolyn, Laura, Malinda, and I decorated some balloons and hung two on John and Mae's door, two on Esther and Mary's door, and two on Dan and Gladys' door. It scared Mae witless when she opened the door the next morning. She thought we girls were responsible, declaring that it's time for paybacks.

Dan read off what I'd written on one of their balloons. I'd written down ten things, the tenth one saying I hope they have a great day. He said he has a reward for the person who did it because it made his day. I asked Mae what made the difference in their responses, but she couldn't explain it.

We are in Minot, North Dakota, having gone 418 miles today.

The measure of a man is what he would be if he never would be found out.

We started off through the rolling countryside of North Dakota.

Grain bins are sprinkled liberally all over. Barley, corn, and sunflowers fill up the fields.

Marvin took a country road to an out of the way truck stop. Not far away was a little fruit stand. Some of the others wandered down that way and came back with some fresh sweet cherries and nectarines. They were kindhearted enough to share the cherries with the rest of us. Fresh fruit: yummy!

In Jamestown, North Dakota, we visited the national Buffalo museum. It is a commemoration of the buffalo and its relationship with the Plains Indians. Buffalo teeth, rib bones, horns, items made from buffalo hide, a shovel made from a shoulder bone, spoons and scoops made from horns, a tepee, a mounted albino buffalo, a buffalo skeleton, and much more are on display.

A short distance away is a 46 foot long, 26 foot high statue of a buffalo. Also close by is a frontier village. Most of its buildings are donated and closed off inside. There was room to step in and look around, but that's all. They were furnished just as they would have been 130 years ago. A few, such as the trading post, were filled souvenirs and such for tourists to buy.

On one side of the street are several log cabins, a general store, a school, a church, a trading post complete with overhang and boardwalk, a barbershop, firehouse, law office, bank, and a blacksmith shop.

On the other side are another store, town hall, train station, an insurance office, post office, print shop, dentist office, and sheriff's office with its jail.

One of Jonas Jr's quizzes: How far can you walk into a woods? If you can't guess the answer ask either him or Dan.

Martha got us started on balloon volleyball. Each side of the bus had a balloon to bat all the way to the back then all the way forward again. One person on each seat had to touch it as it went. The team to get their balloon back to the front seat first got that point. The trick was that if your balloon floated out over the aisle, the other team could bat it any way they chose. We soon found out that it worked best to just try to push the balloon on its way instead of hitting it. Red Door-Side won 15-7 over Green Driver-Side.

At lunchtime most of us girls had chosen the same place to eat. Mae told us others that we may not tease her; she and Daniel have a dinner date tomorrow evening. We others all thought that was just splendid and wished them the best.

We are in Maple Grove, Minnesota, having put on 488 miles today. Dinner was at Golden Corral and it was delicious.

Marty had found a place where you can play Whirly-Ball. The guys needed two more players so Steve asked Malinda and me if we wanted to help. Once everyone was there, we signed up and played 5 on 5 for an hour.

The game is rather crazy, called a cross between basketball and lacrosse with a little hockey thrown in for good measure. Plus you play in bumper cars. Sound interesting?

Each player has a short lacrosse racket to catch and throw the plastic 4 inch ball. The target is a backboard ten feet high with a bull's eye square. Oh, yes, don't forget the players are in bumper cars with no brakes. There was only a handle to steer: turn the handle to the left to go to the right and to the right to go left; turn it completely around to back up and around again the opposite way to go forward once more. Confusing and challenging but fun!

Whenever we hit the bull's eye with the ball, and alarm went off and the backboard lit up. Our team was behind. Somehow Marty go hold of an extra ball. Waiting until almost everyone else was down at the other end, he threw it at the target, scoring a point for us. About thirty seconds later the other team scored with the ball we were supposed to be using. I don't think the referee was watching so he didn't notice anything wrong about it.

Aden scored the star point of the night though. He wound up and threw the ball toward the backboard. The ball flew over the board, bounced off the wall, and hit the back side of the backboard hard enough to set off the alarm and lights for a point. All of us were so surprised that we just looked at the board and laughed.

When our hour was up, we discovered that the rest of the girls had joined Wilma in watching us. They all declared it was hilarious to watch us.

Don't cry because it's over; smile because it happened.

On our way to the Wisconsin Dells this morning, Moses had gone up front to visit with Marvin. Fannie deserted her seat to sit beside Amy. Joe donned her kooky looking curly red wig, hat, and weird glasses, and bulbous nose. After the laughter died down, Steve borrowed the stuff and put it on. He quietly went up behind Emma then stuck his face into hers. She shrieked and jumped six inches off her seat to the great amusement of everyone else.

We had to wait until it was time for our boat tour of the Upper Dells. They are beautiful. The river is edged by bluffs and outcrops of contoured, layered rock. It is a porous rock found in only three other places in the world: Potsdam, New York; Potsdam, Germany; and Zurich, Switzerland. It is soft and porous enough that trees can sink their roots into the rock forty feet down.

One formation looks like the profile of an Indian's head. Kristina, the guide, told us we should appreciate it because it took her six hours to carve it. A narrow channel separates two cliffs called Tall Rock and Romance Rock.

One island in the river is said to have every tree native to Wisconsin growing on it. The Giant's Shield is a huge shield shaped rock standing upright against the riverbank. It is used as the marker for the river's water level. The highest recorded mark was in the 1930's at four feet above the shield. Another island is almond shaped and called Steamboat Rock. It does resemble a steamboat if you look at it with a little imagination.

We got off and walked the planks through Witches Gulch. It is a gorge cut and eroded by water which still splashes and gurgles below the boardwalk. At one point the gulch is narrow with curved, rounded, layered rocks and cliff walls. Pretty Awesome!

Stand Rock was the second place where we docked. It is a tall pillar separated from the neighboring cliff by five feet of air. A German shepherd is trained to jump the space twice for every boatload of tourists. In 1895 the man whose photo became the trademark for the Dells had his young son jump the space until he had the perfect photo. It shows the boy in mid air 47 feet off the ground.

A short trail winds around the cliffs back down to the water. Sometimes the trail was hugging the walls, at other times it wound through the forest. Occasionally a ledge hovered over the trail.

When we were back on the bus, Martha passed the mic around for everyone to tell the highlights of the trip. Denali National Park, the cruise to Columbia Glacier on Prince William Sound, halibut fishing, and services at the Mennonite church were some of the ones mentioned most often.

Jonas Jr. said he enjoyed it all except one thing that he is still bummed about. Everyone else chuckled while he told Martha that the next time they plan to go to the mall in Edmonton, they should make sure there's a Cabela's close by for the men!

All of us thanked Marvin and Martha for giving us such a good trip. When the mike got back up to Marvin, he said, "You passengers make a trip successful or not. The good part is that a little leaven goes through the whole lump. On the other hand, a few bad apples can ruin the whole bushel." Amidst the laughter he went on, "There might have been a few rough edged ones in the batch, but the rest of the load could handle them."

We stopped in Rockford, Illinois, having traveled 348 miles on the road. Some of us wrapped up the evening by invading the breakfast room to play games. No one wanted the evening to end because it was our last one together, yet we knew it would, At least we had several more hours together.

FRIDAY, AUGUST 9

Never be afraid to trust and unknown future to a known God.

How lucky I am to have something that makes saying good by so hard.

Our last day. What a trip we had! We made a bunch of new friends, and imprinted lots of memories on our hearts and minds.

Mary and Esther had a driver to take them home from the hotel. They came out to the bus for devotions and a farewell song then waved as we rolled out of the parking lot.

Dan asked me for the third time (once too often!) to consider writing this book. After lunch I told him I would do the writing and type up the manuscript. Beyond that it is up to him to get it published.

When the mic was passed around again today, Marty told us that one evening Crist had wanted something out of the pop machine. What he wanted cost two dollars and the machine refused to take his five dollar bill. So he tried putting his credit card into the slot and got it stuck. He went to the desk clerk for help and he said a serviceman won't be available until the next day to get the card out. We left the next morning before the guy came so they mailed the credit card home.

Emma informed me that I should put stories like that in the book too. Hopefully she meant stories about her too!

We had lunch in Nappanee where Harry and Irvin got off. It was 1:25 when we arrived in Shipshewana. Daniel, we five Millers, Laura, and Carolyn got off there.

Our driver was waiting to take us on home. After we thanked Marvin and Martha again, the boys started loading luggage onto in van. Just before the bus pulled out, Emma motioned Daniel back on the bus. He came back laughing at whatever she had to say.

On the way home he told Steve what it was: "I can tell Steve's not very concerned about the others. He just got on the van and left the rest of the luggage for the other boys to load up!"

This fired Steve up enough that he headed for the phone soon after arriving home. He left a message for Emma, not saying who was calling, "You obviously didn't see me taking the bags and stuffing them in the back over the seat. That was much harder work than just putting them in up front. I was making a sacrifice to do that so the others wouldn't have to lift them so high. And Mary said we saw four elk." Then he hung up.

Emma had asked me earlier how many elk we had seen. I didn't know offhand but looked it up later and had forgotten to tell Emma.

Home! It was good to be home again and see the rest of the family and tell stories. Thank God for all the new friendships we made, the wonders we saw, and all the memories we created.

the end